Grief
the Teacher

The Teacher We Never Wanted with the Lessons Only Love and Loss Can Teach

By *Kat Farace*

Grief the Teacher
The Teacher We Never Wanted—
With the Lessons Only Love and Loss Can Teach
By Kat Farace
ISBN: [insert number]
Printed in the United States of America

Disclaimer

The information provided in this book is for educational and informational purposes only and is not intended as medical, psychological, or mental health advice. This book is not a substitute for professional counseling, therapy, diagnosis, or treatment. Reading this book does not establish a counselor-client, therapist-patient, or medical relationship between the reader and the author. If you are experiencing severe emotional distress, thoughts of self-harm, or a mental health crisis, please seek immediate assistance from a qualified healthcare provider or contact your local emergency services.

The author and publisher disclaim any liability for decisions made based on the information contained in this book. Readers assume full responsibility for their own choices and actions.

Dedication

To my mom and dad,
Bill and Miriam O'Neal-
Your love did not end when your lives did.
It has sustained me, shaped me,
and your legacy now reaches all the way to
your great grandchildren.

Table of Contents

Special Acknowledgements

To my Love John: Thank you for your selfless devotion. Your unwavering belief in me has empowered my dreams to become a reality.

And to my children, Nathan, Eric, and Sarah, who revived my life through unconditional love and meaning when grief left me feeling so lost.

Introduction

Let me begin by saying this: there are no words, when grief hits. There are no books. There are no theories. There are no steps. There is no solution that will allow you to avoid, overcome, get over, not feel, or return to the life you once had with your loved one.

It is true. They have passed. That part of your relationship has shifted.

I acknowledge your deep sorrow—your unrelenting ache for your loved one. I acknowledge the lump in your throat, the pain in your gut, and the fog in your mind that makes no sense of what you are experiencing. You are no longer yourself. You are no longer the person you were. You are someone else—someone who feels like a stranger in your own life.

You didn't want this.
You didn't ask for it.
You may have preferred it was you who passed away instead of your loved one.

But if that were true, they would now be experiencing this suffering you are.
No—wait. I know that's not what you want either. You are trapped now, knowing this burden—this weight, this suffering—is yours to carry.

Grief is all-consuming. It smothers your every thought. It intrudes on every decision. It diminishes you. You can't see yourself anymore. You don't feel yourself. You can't hear yourself think. You are lost—so profoundly lost.

You feel detached from everything around you. You move through the minutes, the hours, the days, the weeks, the months—but time makes no sense. How could so much time have passed when it feels like yesterday, and also like forever, since they've been gone?

Life demands your attention through routines and responsibilities, but you can't feel yourself doing them. You move through the motions, not knowing how you have survived another day.

There is no light.
There is no color.
There isn't even darkness.
There is only gray.

And you feel completely alone.
...But are you?

Our experiences of grief feel deeply personal—as though no one could possibly know how you feel. And I agree with you. While you may resonate with these words, your grief is still yours alone. No one can feel it exactly as you do. I know this because no one knew how I felt. *No one.*

There is a reason for this. Your relationship with your loved one was uniquely yours—two personalities intertwined through conversations, touches, experiences, and unspoken moments.

For example, imagine you and your twin sibling both losing your mother. Though you share a bond and similarities, each of you had private conversations, personal hugs, and individual moments with her that belonged only to you. Your relationship was yours. And so your grief is uniquely yours. It is unlike any other.

We all grieve alone... together.

This also explains why, as a human race, we struggle so deeply to support one another through grief. We avoid the conversation. We look away. We hesitate to speak the name of the deceased, afraid it will awaken feelings we don't want to feel.

God forbid tears are shed—what would we say then?

The awkwardness of grief is intense. Death and grief have been boxed up and labeled *morbid, too sad, depressing,* or *best avoided.* In doing so, we strip ourselves of the opportunity to love one another through one of the most profound shared experiences of being human.

And that, my friends, is the deepest wound of all.

In this book, we will explore the feelings, experiences, beliefs, traditions, and outcomes of grief. We will turn over ground that may feel unfamiliar and unsteady, examining lessons, perspectives, and possibilities for your life now.

Yes—I'm going to say it.
Your life will never be the same.
It will be transformed.

You weren't looking for it. But you cannot go back. You cannot be who you were. You cannot live in the past, though you may try. It won't work.

Grief is the teacher you never wanted—for the lessons we all need to learn. Lessons in love and life.

These lessons are deep, soul-searching, and unexpected. If you allow them, they can expand your life rather than narrow it. I won't say *better*— although in time it can be. It feels too harsh to think of anything being better than having our loved ones here.

But I will say *impressive.*

Grief can impress upon you a depth of love, perspective, and humanity that you could never have imagined without this experience. If you are willing to decipher the understanding you long for.

You are showing tremendous courage by being willing to examine your grief and search for meaning within your suffering. I hope I can offer light through the echoes of my own grief and the lessons I continue to learn.

We never finish this work. We never get it all right.

This book is not about doing 'right' -but allowing it to teach, with reflections, stories, guidance and even more questions. Having honest conversations—free from fear, tradition, and silence—are worth having, not only for ourselves, but for generations to come.

Thank you for being here.

Please accept my heartfelt sympathy as we walk this shared path alone... together.

Lesson 1
Class Begins

There is a shift that takes place at the very core of your being when you experience the death of someone who played a significant role in the story of your life. If your life were written out like a story, you would see your loved one as a central character—someone who contributed daily to your activities, conversations, decisions, expressions, and experiences. Whether present or remote their impact was felt.

Your senses were shaped by your interactions with them: how they felt to touch, how they smelled, what you heard in their voice, and what you saw in their presence. Those are just the nuances of your relationship. Your conversations, the collaboration of your souls, and day-to-day distractions that moved your emotions to love. They were an important and valuable part of your programming—how you thought about life and thought about: past, present, and future.

Now that they are no longer physically present, so much of what once felt important—managing daily activities, events, special invitations, or the enormous expectations life places on us—has shifted. In some cases, you may now be taking on more responsibilities in your loved one's absence, while letting go of others that are no longer necessary.

Often, this shift casts a shadow so dense that your sense of self becomes depleted. This shift frequently goes invalidated and is often unnoticed, as you try to maintain some recollection of normalcy. But for you, what was once important suddenly appears to no longer matter.

The flip side of this shift is the lesson that what once seemed less urgent can become non-negotiable for your future. Routine health examinations to minimize your chances of dying from the same diagnosis that took your loved one's life. Checking the mechanics of your vehicle, to lesson the risk of a tragic accident. Ensuring a designated driver for yourself or those you care about when socializing. Always—without fail—saying *I love you*. Being mindful of the words you choose when someone walks out your door.

These shifts in your activities, behaviors, priorities, and even the way you think about life itself hold valuable lessons that grief will teach you. You are being changed. Some changes you will embrace. Others will feel unbearably heavy until you begin to crumble under the weight of the new challenges you carry. Finding yourself having to rebuild your life on your own.

Yes— on your own. Even though you may have supportive family and friends around. Because the choice to rebuild can only be done by you.

That crumbling brings yet another shift. You learn that you cannot do it all. You need help. You may change from the strong, independent person you once prided yourself on being to someone who allows others to support you—or who allows certain things to fall apart because you simply can't hold them together anymore. You may even need to leave the beloved home you once shared with your partner because you can no longer maintain it alone.

In every scenario, countless decisions must be made. On one hand, you are in deep sorrow, feeling the pressure to make decisions through the dimmed lens of grief. It can be frightening, to say the least. Yet on the other hand, when you make a choice—no matter how difficult or reluctant—you learn something from your Grief Teacher: that the belief *you cannot move forward without your loved one* is **not** true. You can, and you do.

This forward movement may happen one moment at a time, but it is still movement. Your progress will feel subtle because it is hard to see through the clouds of grief—like driving through dense fog on a mountain road. But you are moving forward. You have no choice.

The Grief Teacher presents you with a list of what matters now and what does not. Some choose not to look at that list. They refuse help and attempt to carry everything alone. This path often damages both the person and their remaining relationships.

Choosing to live as much in the past as possible—refusing to allow grief to teach you, all in the name of never wanting to forget your loved one (as if that were possible)—will affect every fiber of your being. This too is a transformation, but one of decay. Physical health can deteriorate. Mental health can decline. Other relationships are neglected. You will not be the same—only now, the loss is far greater.

Letting go of resistance to the Grief Teacher allows a natural flow. The road will be rugged. You will cry more tears than you ever imagined, to the point of exhaustion and even irritation. You will feel the stench of grief so deeply that you will long for fresh air. Yet grief, in its natural and progressive way, will show you life as you never expected.

Your priorities will change. You will value time more and how you spend it. You will see yourself, your relationships, your beliefs, your health, your money, and your experiences differently. You will become more tolerant of some things and less for others. You will recognize the importance of self-care. You will love from a new perspective—one larger than you have ever known. You will develop an eternal point of view.

Grief, the teacher, reveals everything we once took for granted. Everything we believed held such importance. The things we stressed over, stole excessive amounts of time for, and believed could never be put aside. All of that wasted energy is dismantled by grief's simple argument: your time, your health, and your choices for life are worth more.

Grief is a teacher—when you let down your resistance. Not the attacker, it is believed to be.

Moving forward, you can gain clarity about the strongholds in your life—what to release and what to hold tightly. What has lasting value and what is ultimately meaningless.

If only life could have taught me these lessons without requiring such sorrow. The truth is, sadly, I wouldn't have listened. I couldn't have. As a society—within families, communities, friendships, and intimate relationships—we are taught from a very young age not to talk about death or grief. We do not examine the natural occurrence of death and grief. It's "too uncomfortable." So we stay silently in our suffering. Holding back the lessons every human needs to learn. That silence became the greatest obstacle in my grief journey.

Where My Story Began

I was eleven when I experienced my first death. It was my Auntie Jo—MaryJo—my mother's sister. They were very close. I often went to her house, which felt magical to me. There were trees to climb—one even had a swing. She would set me up in her kitchen nook with an apron and watercolors, where I could explore how colors blended across a canvas board.

A few months before her death, I wasn't allowed to visit anymore. When I asked to go, my mom would say, *Auntie Jo wasn't feeling well and we will go when she feels better*—then the subject would abruptly change. I could feel the sadness. The energy in the room collapsed whenever her name was mentioned. My mother would walk away, wiping her eyes believing I didn't notice the pool of tears.

I believe my mother thought she was protecting me from painful information by pretending everything was fine when the unspoken truth was— *your aunt has cancer and might not survive.* Looking back, she was likely protecting herself from a conversation filled with fear and disbelief. All I know is that the absence of conversation left me alone with my thoughts. What could have been moments of love, shared compassion, and connection were replaced by silence—and silence carried its own pain, amplified by loneliness, confusion and distance.

It was Halloween. I still hadn't chosen a costume. I went looking for my mom and noticed her bedroom door was closed, which was unusual. I quietly cracked it open and saw her sitting on the bed, sobbing. I closed the door quickly and ran to my room. I had never seen my mother cry like that before.

Later, my dad told me we wouldn't be going trick-or-treating that night. No explanation— just the fact. I replied, "That's okay, Daddy, I don't have a costume anyway" pretending everything was fine, just as I had been taught. A few days later, I overheard that Auntie Jo had died. She died that Halloween. I'm not sure I even understood what that fully meant. Other than comparing it with my pet gold fish, I had never experienced a death. The weight of this reality was lost on me and would take time for me to grasp the impact.

The tragedy was never discussed. I assume there was a funeral, but I wasn't aware of it. I went to school as though nothing had happened. Yet I noticed the dark cloud of mourning in our home—and the casseroles from neighbors and church friends. I felt alone, confused, and a little scared—the very emotions my mother was trying to protect me from, now intensified by silence. There was never a moment that someone said to me directly — *your Auntie Jo died.*

My grandmother died a year later. I knew she was sick after suffering a stroke when I was 10. My mom took me to the nursing home every day after school to visit. Grandma no longer recognized me. When I asked what was wrong with Grandma,, my mom said, "She has dementia," and immediately changed the subject—again reinforcing that these things were not to be discussed. Dementia was never explained to me, but I concluded at that time, when you hit your seventies, you go back to being a child and forget everything. Without a conversation, I assumed this is how the end of life was for everyone, if you live long enough to be old.

A few weeks went by and I didn't get to go with my mom to visit grandma. I knew what was coming. It was just like Auntie Jo. No words spoken. Visits ended and my mama wiping the tears from her eyes. This time however I was told— "Grandma is now with Jesus in Heaven." It was presented as a good thing which was of course confusing because everyone was so sad. I asked no questions. Apparently, being a year older afforded me the opportunity to learn more about death as the conversations around me were not hidden and I went to the funeral. Maybe it was because Grandma was older so her death was more expected.

Honestly Grandma's death felt like it happened before Auntie Jo's because the fun visits to her little crooked house, and rides to Clifton's Cafeteria for lunch in her 54 pink Chevy stopped immediately after her stroke. She seemed like a shell. She looked like my Grandma but nothing else about her was the same.

My grandmother was the first dead body I ever saw. At the funeral home, I sat quietly in the corner. Someone said, "Doesn't she look peaceful? Like she's asleep." Inside, I thought, *are you crazy? That doesn't look like my grandma at all.* She looked blue, rubbery and she never wore make-up before. I silently smiled anyway, pretending everything was fine—just like everyone else in the room.

A year later, my mother was diagnosed with cancer—the word that was never spoken aloud in our home. I learned this fact through overheard conversations and paperwork I wasn't meant to see on our dining room table. Her journey was long and brutal. Radiation. Chemotherapy. Surgery. Remission. More treatments, more surgery. It became common all through my teenage years. Meanwhile, my dad suffered two heart attacks in the midst of Mama's treatments. Somewhere during these years I think my brother started using drugs to cope. None of these things were discussed. If you don't ask questions, then you don't have to hear about the bad stuff—so only necessary facts were stated. We kept to routines, silent smiles, hugs, and light verbal exchanges to keep the status quo.

Every adult I knew participated in this masquerade with our family. Their pity hid behind trivial conversations and constant reassurances that "everything is fine." I became excellent at pretending. None of my friends knew what was happening. I rarely spoke a word of the chaos I was living to any of my childhood friends. The few times it came up, no one knew what to say or how to respond. So the subject was quickly changed. My parents loved me deeply, and their intentions were good to keep me from the horrors of long-term terminal illness. They did the best they knew how. I understand that more clearly now. But the effects of this charade affected me in ways I'm still discovering.

Instead of learning from Grief—the honest teacher—I learned from *Avoidance*, a ruthless guide that nearly destroyed me as the years continued on. Grief may be the teacher you never wanted, but avoidance will hollow you out until you feel invisible.

Grief did eventually become my teacher decades later. It had relentlessly pursued me. From age eleven to thirty, I experienced fourteen deaths; aunts, uncles, my grandparents, a cousin two friends and both of my parents. I resisted grief naturally, as most do. I practiced avoidance and pretending because that is what I had been taught. My life had shifted beyond my control, and I resisted to move with it.

It is important to note that my parents were the kindest, most well-intended people I have ever known. They adopted me when I was 3 months old. Their unconditional love was obvious to me, and they were protective to a fault. I was comfortable in our little 3-bedroom home even though the harsh realities of life were beating us all to a pulp. Kindness was a standard, but raw discussion or preparation about how to manage the cruelties of life was dismissed.

Had I been allowed to feel my grief earlier, I might have avoided choices rooted in fear—choices that led to chronic illness through self-neglect and remaining in damaging relationships where I learned to placate rather than be whole. Perhaps I would have taught my own children better how to navigate the difficult challenges in their lives. Pain cannot be avoided; we just pretend it can.

Once I started to surrender to my Grief Teacher, I learned about the importance of *now*. Of seeing the truth in situations, of time, self-care, compassion, and sharing your words no matter how raw or sad. I learned that love does not end with death.

Listen to Your Teacher
The longing you feel for your loved one shows you how big love is.
Your loneliness reveals the importance of connection with yourself, and with others.
Your tears remind you that pain softens when tears are allowed.
Pain can be relieved with less resistance and a good cry.
Peace can be found when nothing makes sense and you quiet your mind long enough to hear your heart.
Grief teaches you that *you* matter—and that tending to yourself is not selfish, but necessary.

Grief teaches you that your relationship with your loved one who has died is unbreakable. It continues and can make a profound difference for your daily experiences, how you express yourself, how you view yourself, and how you view others that you love. When you speak your grief, you create possibilities for yourself and others that can be life-changing. Not just in sorrow but in revelation of life.

It is up to you now to choose your next step in your grief work. Which direction will go?

Lesson 2
Learning the Hard Way

There are two ways to ride a roller coaster.
One: Gripped with fear.
Two: Letting go and going with the flow.

Let's look at the first choice.

You wait in line—sometimes for hours. With each passing moment, you inch through a line in a maze, listening again and again to the screams of those ahead of you as they fly by on a ride designed to excite and terrify. You pretend it's cool, no big deal. You go through the motions while your heart begins to pound so loudly you're sure everyone can hear it—and see how scared you are becoming.

You notice how the carts clunk, creak, and vibrate. There's that awful grinding sound as the train of small bench seats, complete with metal bar restraints, climbs the steepest hill. The coaster's victims chug upward as if their combined weight is too much for the tiny, barely secured wheels struggling to pull the heavy train forward. It feels painfully obvious that this thing is unsafe, yet you ignore common sense and try to look brave for the people you're with.

It's your turn.

You want to walk away, but you can't. It feels impossible. There's no way out but through. Others around you are smiling, joyfully excited—either oblivious to the perceived threat to life or deeply avoiding it. Meanwhile, you feel like you might vomit or at least pee your pants. You're sweating and dizzy, and you haven't even reached the worst part yet.

You're strapped into the death carriage now, and some teenager demonstrates just how much *flex* there is in the safety bar—only confirming your worst fears. Once you reach the top, you're convinced you'll be launched forward and tumble out through the slack in the bars, or worse, get stuck upside down, dangling like a fish on the end of a line. So you grip the bar tighter, grit your teeth, bow your head, and pray: *Oh God, oh God, oh God oh God*. And off you go. Your stomach is in your throat. You can't see anything clearly. You have no idea where you're headed or how it will end.

Sound familiar? Yep. That's just like grief.

Grief with resistance is just like that roller coaster ride. The more you resist, the harder it becomes—the ups and downs, sharp turns, loops, and sudden drops. The mental games that play in your head. The constant sense of insecurity. The unbearable weight of it all. The fear that you won't survive. It can feel as though the bottom has completely dropped out.

I've spoken with thousands of people over decades who describe their grief in remarkably similar ways. The ride itself doesn't change. The lack of security, the whiplash thoughts, circumstantial jolts, physical suffering, mental uncertainty, waves of fear and the feeling that life is nearly over—these are universal parts of everyone's ride.

One of the greatest falsehoods your resistance to grief convinces you of, is that you have no control. None. Zero. Zip. You've been forced onto this roller coaster, and there is no getting off. You must endure every hill, turn, loop, and plunge. The ride lasts longer than expected, and the outcome feels completely uncertain. Even now you may be clinging to what feels like a flimsy safety handle—and you are losing your grip.

Grief comes with many symptoms. Some you expect. Others catch you completely off guard. You never knew this depth of pain was possible to feel. Most people describe it as the most excruciating pain and suffering they've ever experienced. I completely agree. Because the experience is so foreign, you may not have words for it—certainly no roadmap. No evidence of the gaping wound. That's why you feel out of control. Because you are.

This would be a good time to pause for a solid cry.
But come back—we still need to find your way through.

Did you know the odds of dying on a roller coaster are about **1 in 750 million**?* Those are excellent odds. In comparison, even better: there is a **0% chance you will die from grief itself**. However, studies show an **88% increased risk of death within ten years** for individuals experiencing high, unrelenting, and unaddressed grief.** Underline here <u>unaddressed.</u> (*Credit- IAAPA and NSC. **Credit- research team led by Mette Kjaegaard Nielson/Aarhus University.)

Grief is not the cause of death, but the intense stress it produces can lead to serious health conditions—cardiovascular disease, immune system suppression, or what is known as broken heart syndrome (*takotsubo cardiomyopathy*). People under chronic grief-related stress may also engage in unhealthy behaviors such as reduced exercise, over eating, under eating, increased substance use, risky behaviors, or neglecting self-care, which can lead to clinical depression and more.

Stress—not grief—is what defeats you. Grief is a Teacher.

It's estimated that **2.8 million deaths worldwide each year** are related to stress and stress-induced illnesses by the International Labour Organization (ILO). You will not die from grief, but if you neglect it and resist its lessons, you may suffer deeply from the stress of loss—and those odds are not good.

So what's the second way to ride the roller coaster? You're already out of control—so no resistance. Go with the flow. If you want to cry, cry. If you want to scream, scream. If you want to talk about it, *talk about it.*

I've ridden the coaster both ways. I've white-knuckled it, certain I would not make it out alive. I've also ridden it differently. While waiting in line, I noticed the shared laughter and the way people boarded in groups, comforting one another as they strapped in. The ride itself didn't change—every turn, loop, and drop was still there—but the approach was entirely different.

Hands flew into the air as the coaster plunged, climbed, and flipped upside down. Letting go and trusting the movement taught me something: on a roller coaster, there is always motion. You are moving through it. There is always relief after the hardest part. And from the highest points, there is a broader perspective.

Grief, my teacher, tried to show me the same truth. I instinctively wanted to let go—to allow my feelings to flow, to speak honestly, and to say everything I wanted to say. To accept I was afraid and my feelings of sorrow as they arose rather than avoiding them. The more freedom you give yourself to grieve, the more you'll see that movement is constant, moments of relief do come, and perspective does expand from this revealing ride.

Many people misuse and misunderstand the phrase "let go."

Two weeks after my mother died, my then husband (now ex) said to me while I was crying, "It's been two weeks. You need to get over it and move on. Just let it go." I wanted to punch him and scream, *You get over that, asshole.* I didn't. Instead, I abandoned my Grief Teacher and I sat silently reinforcing my false belief that I needed to hide and suffocate my feelings to make *others* more comfortable.

I'm not suggesting you punch anyone. But I did have other options. I could have expressed how I felt. I could have given myself permission to cry and care for my needs—regardless of others' opinions.

I desperately wanted to talk about my mom with people. Friends, family, strangers—it didn't matter. I had just turned twenty and was emerging from the wreckage of my teenage years. I longed for someone to say my mom's name. To talk about her easygoing personality and dry wit. To laugh about how she wasn't a great cook—but how her stew and butterscotch pie were unforgettable.

But the discomfort on others' faces whenever the topic of mother arose shut me down like a nail in my own coffin. It felt as though my mom wasn't just dead—she had been erased. At her funeral, my ex-mother-in-law said, "It's alright, dear. I'm your mother now."

Umm No! No your not! No way. No how. I'd rather be an orphan.

The audacity of that statement—as if anyone could so easily fill my mom's shoes that were still by her bedside while she was lying in a casket across from us. Unfathomable. Unbearable. Sadly, unselfishly, regretfully, I responded, "Okay, thank you." My resistance, silence, and avoidance made a liar out of me, too.

I knew all along that what I was doing was wrong. I could feel grief exploding inside me, begging for release. Pressuring me to share how I truly felt. The Teacher wanted me to let it all go. That is what "let go" truly means—not letting go of your loved one's memory, but letting go of false beliefs about grief and death. Letting go of the fear of feeling your sorrow. Letting yourself cry, yell, and fall apart. Giving time and space for grief to make itself known.

You will stop eventually. It may take days, weeks, or months. Continued expressions will go on for years—but your response to grief must be honest.

Talk to people. Share what you are feeling. It's time to *let go* of the harmful ways we handle grief out of fear. Stop the self-sabotage. Grief, the Teacher, is inviting you to let go and go with the flow.

Not everyone will be able to climb on your ride with you. You may only find one or two people who are willing. They may be someone you know or they may be strangers at a support group. There are people who are on the road ahead of you. You don't have to ride the coaster alone.

And here is the truth grief teaches clearly: You are never meant to let go of your loved one. **You keep their spirit alive in you.** The exchanges you had with them impacted you. So carry them forward—every memory, every meaningful conversation, the laughs that made you cry, the arguments you managed to love each other through, silent moments, and shared pain. The tender touches and redundant routines all matter. The relationship doesn't end. It changes.

It is different now. It has transitioned. But it is not dead. Your relationship is not dead. Letting go of what blocks your grief and its lessons allows you to hold tightly to what truly matters.

Once grief has arrived, the next lesson is not whether you can stop the ride – but how you choose to experience it.

Lesson 3
Changing Classrooms

Shortly after my sweet mama died, my dad died too. Not physically—not until nine years later—but when my mom died, something inside him died immediately. It was traumatic, visible, and reactive. From the moment he left her bedside at the hospital, he was never the same.

He saw it coming, I'm sure. He had participated in the charade of pretending everything would be okay, but when she died, he decided it would never be okay again. He stopped pretending. And without the skills, knowledge, or resilience to cope, he became a victim of a grief tsunami that slowly suffocated him over time—quite literally.

Frankly, I had no idea what had just happened.

My mom had been at the City of Hope in Duarte, California, for a few weeks. I went there directly after work every day to spend the evening with her, bringing food that sounded appealing. She could only take a bite or two, but I didn't care—as long as she ate something she wanted.

I don't remember our conversations clearly. We talked a lot, but never about what was happening to her. We just talked about nothing in particular. I even got reprimanded at work for calling her a couple of times each day during work hours. This was 1981, so I had to use the company phone. I told my boss my mom was in the hospital, and she allowed me to call once a day briefly to see if my mom needed anything before I headed over.

I never told my boss that my mom had cancer or was dying—because I didn't believe she was. She had always come home from the hospital before. I was sure she would again.

This routine felt normal. My parents had been hospitalized many times over the years, so this wasn't new. I knew my mom was weak, losing weight, sleeping more, and barely eating—but not a single person, not family, friends, clergy, or hospital staff, ever told me these were signs of actively dying.

I thought it was just another bad spell. Eventually, she would rally. Feel a little stronger, eat a little more, and do a little more.

She always did. My mom was a fighter. And I
was an expert pretender.

I Didn't See It Coming

It was the final game of the MLB (Major League
Baseball) World Series—our home team, the LA
Dodgers, playing against the New York Yankees.
The game was showing on a tiny black-and-
white television mounted from the ceiling at the
other end of the room above my mom's bed. The
picture was fuzzy, barely watchable, but we
turned it up like it was the radio and listened to
each play. Which was appropriate for this family
of avoiders.

My dad was there. My husband (now ex).
My brother. Two of my uncles—my mom's
brothers—and two of her closest friends. Others
came in and out to say *hi*. They were actually
saying goodbye, but I refused to see it. I viewed
it instead as a beautiful outpouring of love while
my mom was hospitalized—again. No final
words of goodbye were spoken, just I love you
and we will see you soon.

I sat on the bed and leaned back, her head
resting on my shoulder. Her eyes were closed as
she took small licks of a cherry popsicle I held
for her. She drifted softly to sleep, red lips and
all. At the end of the game, I tried to rouse her.
"Mom, we won! The Dodgers won the World
Series!" I saw an impish grin of I thought... an
acknowledgment, but she never spoke another
word.

If I had known—if I had understood—if someone had told me this was it, I would have paid attention. I know she said a few things that night. Very few. But I didn't grasp the severity of the moment. Though I had experienced death in my family before, I had never witnessed one. She was my first of many.

I hated that I didn't know what her last words were. I was confident they would have such meaning to me. Overtime I learned that her last words were not important. It was all the exchanges we had in our life time together that mattered. That's what our relationship was built on not the last thing she would have said. Our love was so much bigger than a few words uttered before she died.

Eventually, everyone left except my dad, my husband, and me. I didn't want to leave until my dad did. My dad seemed especially sad, though he denied it, saying he was just tired. Pretending everything was ok.

Nurses came in periodically to check my mom's vitals. Staff members stopped by to say *hi*—really, goodbye—because they all knew her from years of treatments and hospitalizations. Everyone loved my mom. Visiting hours ended, but no one rushed us out. My dad had worked at City of Hope for years as part of the janitorial staff, so we felt like extended family. I was sure that was why they let us stay.

It grew late. I moved from the bed to a wooden chair beneath the teetering television, rested my head in my hand, and dozed off. My sleep was broken with the sounds of passersby in the hospital hall and the continued checks from the nursing staff. Other than that, we all managed to catch a few winks while my mom appeared to lie comfortably in the bed. No movement. No noise other than the pace of labored breathing through the oxygen mask.

Near 7 a.m., I startled awake. Several nurses surrounded my mom. Others were consoling my dad, who stood motionless—tears streaming down his face, no sound escaping him. Neither did my mom. I stared at her chest, waiting—pleading—for it to rise and fall.

Come on, Mom... breathe, breathe.
She didn't. She was lifeless.
A nurse looked at me gently, pitifully, and said, "I'm so sorry."

If I could insert a thousand blank pages here, they would perfectly describe how I felt. Blank. Blank. Blank. Blank. Empty. No words. No thoughts. No tears. No reaction. Just blank.

How could this have happened?

I don't remember what happened next. I had driven myself to the hospital the night before. So I know I had to drive myself home. I remember getting into my mini truck. I remember pulling out of the parking lot. I remember being on the freeway. I don't remember the drive. I don't remember where I went. I don't remember where my dad was. Should I have even been driving? Probably not.

Shock set in for days—like a violent storm with high winds and flash flooding. For the next few days after Mama died, people gathered at the small three-bedroom house I grew up in. I was furious when I heard many of them already discussing which of my mom's belongings they would like to have to remember her by. My mom was a collector of Hummel's and antiques, and she had some wonderful pieces. My dad, who rarely got upset, finally snapped. "No. Don't touch anything."

They could have taken everything for all I cared. I didn't want her things. I wanted my mom. How could anyone be talking about *things*?

I knew what death was. I had seen what it did to my family before. But this grief was different. How had I been so blind that I didn't even allow myself to realize my mom was dying? Why didn't anyone talk to me? I was young—

married but still a girl, really. Why did no one tell me what was happening to the most important person in my life?

I was lost. I was furious.

Resilience is defined as the capacity to withstand or recover from difficulty. It's considered a virtue. I stepped right up, just as I had been taught. Swallow your feelings. Do what needs to be done.

I planned the funeral, chose the casket, and made most of the arrangements. My dad was present for all but absent of mind. I ran everything by him, but he couldn't—or wouldn't—make decisions. He left it all to me and anyone else in our family with an opinion. I have no recollection of what my brother was doing during this process. My cousin Angie was a great support and I was grateful for her presence. My mom was loved by so many and I was surrounded by kindness, but ultimately I felt the responsibility was mine to hold it together.

Dad was not resilient. He chose to get lost in his grief, lost in her memory, trapped in the past, and he never returned to the joyful, loving man I grew up with. I lost both parents in one fell swoop—one to death, the other to grief.

I never told anyone how angry I was. Not a soul knew my rage—for decades. That to me was bravery. That was resilience, as I had been taught. "Put up and shut up." Avoid. Pretend. And people praised me for it.

But the truth was, I was burying my soul like my dad—only I was better at it, because nobody knew.

I grew up in the Pentecostal Foursquare Christian faith. Church wasn't once a week—it was most of the week. Three services on Sunday. Bible study Wednesday. Choir Thursday. Home groups. Saturday events. My dad was the church janitor, so even on off days, I was there cleaning bathrooms, vacuuming carpets, and dusting furniture, while my dad buffered floors, reset furniture and took out the trash. I felt like we were there more than we weren't.

Faith is supposed to bring comfort. But my Grief Teacher whispered something different: *It's okay to be angry. God can handle it.*

Instead, I practiced what I now call faux resilience—smiling, comforting others, and suppressing myself.

My one act of rebellion? I wore white to my mom's funeral. Everyone else wore black or navy. I said my mom was in heaven, happy and healed, and I would honor that truth in white. The church folks praised my bravery. My dad's side of the family thought I'd lost my mind.

I didn't care. I was angry. I didn't want to play by the rules. I didn't want to wear black—or white. I didn't want to be there at all. My faux resilience dragged me through every nauseating step of the way.

Grief teaches resilience—but not the fake kind.

True resilience comes from honesty. From allowing vulnerability. From letting others help. From acknowledging weakness without shame. Handling everything alone keeps you trapped—like a hamster on a wheel—convinced your sorrow is the end of your life. It feels like hopelessness. Loneliness and longing are all you will ever know, and you maintain the mantra, *I will never get over grief.* And now that statement has become societies banner for those who grieve. A doomsday message, that you adopt as your own.

Resilience does not mean *getting over your loss*. It does not mean you bounce back and forget, or that the significance of the relationship has less value because you *feel better*. It means recovering from each wave of grief. And there will be many waves. And you can recover, catch breath and move forward. You can learn how to handle each wave. Recognize what it is upon approach. Give yourself the space to go the flow and feel relief.

Just as your body signals fatigue or illness and requires care, grief signals emotional and physical pain that needs attention. When you respond with gentleness and self-care, recovery follows. When you ignore it, suffering deepens.

For example, you are home alone sitting in a chair your loved one once occupied, watching meaningless television when you feel the ache in your chest from the gaping hole in your heart. Tears begin to swell in your eyes, and you think, *I can't do this without them.* Your unattended thoughts multiply, and before you can catch a breath, you are sobbing uncontrollably in your pillow—again.

What was the first feeling? Ache in your chest. You know what that means and where it leads. What if you acknowledged it by saying aloud, *I miss you?* Then quietly listen to your inner voice at that moment. Give space to that initial grief symptom. Press into your relationship. You will feel them loving you immediately, and you might even hear the response, not audibly, but in your heart—*I'm right here.* (More on this later.)

Without this nurturing attention to the first indication of grief, that moment of pain gains momentum. Your thoughts compound and your suffering expands. The wave consumes you and you tumble around looking for ground and air.

Grief Symptoms

Your loved one dies. You have deep sorrow. Shock, denial, uncontrolled crying, fatigue, restlessness, looping thoughts, longing, loneliness, anxiety, depression, physical pain, mental instability, indecisiveness, forgetfulness, anger, and so much more. These are symptoms, reactions, and indicators that you are grieving. They are normal responses and expected. You may not experience all of them, but you will experience a lot of them.

The waves come like hurricanes— they can be blinding, violent, and disorienting. You can't see land. But it's there. The path exists, even when hidden by the storm. Take hope in knowing that and take down the banner, *I will never get over grief.*

When grief indicators arise, they are not just reminders of death—they are signals from your whole being asking for care. When you tend to them early, you reduce the damage and prevent the tsunami that swallowed my dad.

I was angry—at everyone. At God. At myself. And instead of listening, I pretended I was fine. I fulfilled responsibilities. I pleased others. And it cost me dearly—my health, my sense of self, and many years of poor decisions. If I had listened to my Grief Teacher—processed my anger, sought support, which would have honored my bond with my mom, I would have learned true resilience. A resilience that would have served me the rest of my life.

*And here is what I mean by pressing **into** that relationship.*

I have always felt my parents' presence since they died. Despite what I was taught, I knew they were only physically gone. My mom's love seemed as if it was expanding. I felt her presence guiding me. Comforting me. Validating me.

I felt her approval for wearing white to her funeral, and she seemed supportive of my anger. Not consoling but substantiating my hidden feelings. It was not words I could hear but blocks of thought, a knowing that was responding to my concerns. It was as though I was receiving a message from her, from her new perspective. This comfort was contrary to the conforming teachings she had given me in life, but I somehow knew she had *let go* herself.

Her soul was not dead. Our relationship did not end with her death. It is alive and well still today. I dared not to share this with anyone, and it would be decades before I knew that this is an invalidated common occurrence for the bereaved.

Grief was my Teacher

Grief taught me that death is physical, not final. It expands perspective. It invites wiser choices. Resilience is not getting over loss—it is expressing my feelings fully in each moment grief visits. Grief, the Teacher, shows us how life is meant to be lived—moment by moment, with awareness, compassion, and courage. Without fear of death, for life is a continuum just transformed to new realms.

I did not understand the depths of these lessons until grief showed up uninvited. It showed up in ways and poked at every belief and pretense I had fostered. I could not have imagined all the variables of pain ahead.

Lesson 4
Grief Detention

Long after my prolonged years of personal death experiences, I found myself devastated by another kind of grief—grief from divorce. I married at age 18. Since my family was sick and dying, college wasn't even a consideration. Honestly, I really do not recall having any conversations with anyone about what my future would be. My mom married at 18. She and my dad were extremely compatible and very adoring to each other, so naturally that's what I thought I was supposed to do. It was as if I was swimming with a school of fish. You just followed what everyone else before you was doing.

Sadly, my divorce was greatly complicated by betrayal. Not only from my ex-husband but also from some key members of my "church family." The story is long, complex, and deeply painful. While I once believed myself to be an innocent victim of circumstances that sabotaged me, I can now see, from the wiser eyes of grief, that I was also an active participant in allowing abuse to take place. My refusal to address my grief issues from the time I was a little girl set patterns of behavior so ingrained that I didn't realize they would eventually shatter my heart.

I learned to pretend that what was happening right in front of me was not happening at all. I learned to shut down my feelings about sickness, death, and grief, burying them deep inside. I learned to tell people what they wanted to hear to avoid conflict or discomfort of any kind. On the outside, I looked brave. I looked resilient. But inside, I was afraid, small, and invisible.

My unresolved grief led me to treat every obstacle and challenge in my life with blinders on and a forced smile. I could see the train of my marriage speeding toward the edge of a cliff, and instead of dealing with it head-on, by standing up for myself and not allowing myself to be manipulated and mistreated, I turned my back, looked the other way, and pretended everything was ok. It wasn't intentional. It was all I knew how to do. Fear flooded my marital life with a man who could not control his temper.

Perhaps if my family had still been alive, I would have confided in my mom or dad. I know without a doubt that if they had known what was happening behind the closed doors of my home, they would have supported me. But they were gone—so I played my role as a happy, supportive wife.

I am not, in any way, taking the blame for the pain and harm done to me. I am, however, owning the fact that by shutting myself down, ignoring my emotions, denying the truth of my circumstances, and refusing to care for myself, I contributed by opening the door to my suffering. I experienced tragic loss I never expected—hurting both myself and my children in ways I couldn't foresee. While I could blame my childhood trauma for being the pseudo person I was, as an adult the responsibility to heal ultimately became mine. I silenced my inner guidance and instead wore the garment of victim-hood, marching forward in faux resilience and false beliefs. I can see it clearly now. It took the grief of losing everything to learn this lesson from the grief teacher.

I am a valuable, worthy human being—capable of finding myself, expressing myself, and knowing myself. I allowed my circumstances to convince me otherwise and walked straight into traps laid by unresolved grief. I spent my life pretending everything was fine when it was anything but.

You may be thinking, what does all this have to do with grief? In retrospect I can see how the illnesses and deaths in my families' lives and the unattended grief created the framework for how I handled many of my future decisions. I just went along with anybody's opinions. I had my smile on and agreeable responses, while inside I was trying to shut down my screaming thoughts and fears.

If grief had been addressed—if my thoughts, beliefs, and emotions had been allowed to be shared and given time and space to heal—perhaps I would have learned the importance of self-care and that my thoughts, feelings, and emotions had value. What if my mom told me how she felt when her sister died, when her mother died, and when she was diagnosed? Yes, it would have been sad, difficult, and painful, but it would have also made room for a deeper unconditional love expression between us. The opportunity was there to learn from the harsh realities of our present, which could have been a strong support for my future.

I would have trusted that through all the hardships, I was a survivor—not the victim I believed myself to be. My perspective would not have been limited to the box I lived in labeled *everything is fine*.

Maybe when my ex-husband told me to "get over" my mom's death just two weeks after she died—when the shock was only beginning to wear off and reality of grief cut through me like a dagger—I could have responded with self-care. I should have said, "I will cry as long as I need to." Maybe if I had found someone—anyone—who could have supported me in my grief, I would have known to be stronger. I would have

ignored the discomfort on others' faces and
chosen to speak about my mom anyway. Years
later, if I had listened to the knowing in my
heart that my dad desperately needed help, I
would have confronted his pain instead of
avoiding it. Maybe then my children might have
known the joyful man I knew as a very young
girl. The dad he once was. They met only "sad
dad," not my dad.

My Story of Grief Continues

I was forty years old when I divorced. I had to
leave my home and the only family I had known
in my adult life—my in-laws. I lost my job, my
marriage, my community, and my sense of
belonging. My faith was fractured and opened
up for examination.

This disenfranchised grief began when I was
working for the church—a job I loved. I was the
youth director, planning parties, retreats, and
summer camp and teaching teens, which I
adored. If I had gone to college, I would have
become a teacher. This job held similarities of
that role for me. As a little girl, I used to playact
that I was a teacher when I was alone in my
bedroom. This job was a perfect fit. I could be
present for my kids, serve a church I loved, and
earn supplemental income that eased tension at
home.

One day, I was called into the pastor's office.
I smiled, assuming the meeting was about the
summer camp I was planning—on schedule,

under budget, and well organized. Instead, the pastor bluntly asked for my resignation. I was confused by his statement. He gave no clear reason and assured me that he had not received any complaints from parents or kids about me. He even confirmed that I was well loved. When pressed, he flippantly said I wasn't organized enough—an accusation completely untrue. My work was thorough, frugal and documented. Which is why I was chosen to be the Dean of youth summer camp including 5 other churches.

I knew something was being hidden. Something the pastor was completely unwilling to address with me. When I refused to resign without a good reason, he fired me on the spot.

I was shocked. I sobbed all the way home and had no idea how I was going to explain this to my kids and their dad. I felt utterly humiliated. However, I still was the Dean of Summer Camp and was allowed to complete this task, as I had organized the whole thing. We had hundreds of kids coming. I was in charge and it was only weeks away. With a big smile on my face, I faked my way through every heartbreaking moment.

While I am not a big fan of labels, the term 'disenfranchised grief' was the perfect term to describe my experience. It is grief that isn't openly acknowledged, publicly mourned or socially supported. People around you do not acknowledge that you are grieving when you go through the loss of a job, home, or marriage.

You do not receive the concession of support as you would from a death loss.

Months later, I learned the truth: Unknown to me, my husband's illicit behavior had been exposed. The church could not legally fire me for his actions, so they fabricated a reason. Had they told me the truth, I would have resigned immediately. The secrecy caused unnecessary devastation. My life became a church scandal—a grief with no casseroles, no sympathy, and no safe place to land.

Once the truth was exposed, I started lining up my ducks and preparing for a divorce. Six months later I waited for my husband to go to work. Immediately after, I picked up the U-Haul I had on hold. I moved out of my beautiful 5-bedroom home with my three kids into a tiny 3-bedroom rental. The divorce was not amicable. I was terrified, having never lived on my own, not to mention the responsibility of parenting my 3 very hurt kids.

Divorce grief is different. It lingers. It resurfaces in run-ins with your ex at the grocery store, shared friendships become awkward, and forced encounters uncomfortable. It isn't worse than death—but it is its own kind of loss. And grief, by then, was my constant companion. I knew how to handle it—or so I thought. Blinders on. Smile in place.

At forty, and no college degree, I had to rebuild. I found work in hospice—supporting dying patients and grieving families. Ironically, I became the person I once needed. I excelled. I was promoted. Others told me I had found my calling. But inside, I was hard, cold —denying my own grief a voice.

I understood, respected, and valued my work, but I hated the job. Every day, grief, either mine or my clients', confronted me. Triggers of my own unattended grief were constant. After years of success but paired with inner collapse, I broke. Grief had finally grabbed me by the heart and shook me around like a rag doll. I couldn't control my tears. I cried constantly—before work, after work, and in between my client visits. Instead of admitting to anyone at work what I was going through, I would tell coworkers I had allergies to explain the ever flowing tears. My employer didn't want me to leave, and they couldn't afford to. I had taken on the responsibility of three different roles, while being paid for one. My faux resilience had an upside to employers as I was definitely an overachiever with a need to be approved of. But I was really just a big mess. My smiling costume was falling apart.

There was nowhere left to run. I couldn't hide, fake, or pretend my way through this grief any longer. I had to go through it.

Grieving requires safety—a place to be seen, heard, and supported. Had I been given that as a child and in my young adult life, I would have lived more authentically. One person offering, in subtle but persistent terms, *Let's talk about it,* would have allowed me to release the pressure. When I work with children and adults, I immediately confront their concerns, stating, "*I know this is awkward, I know you don't feel comfortable, and I know you don't want to be here, but I'm willing to listen to anything you want to say.*" And I do. No judgment. No correcting. No advice. Just space for grief.

Grief is not an exception to the rule; it is part of being human. Death, divorce, loss of home, identity, and security—these are all grief encounters shared. Everyone grieves.

Eventually, I realized I needed to give myself the same permission to grieve that I had offered hundreds of others in my work. I turned inward. I listened. I remained open to what is possible. I discovered that love and relationship is not lost nor does it disappear—it transforms.

Grief, my teacher, had followed me everywhere. And through it, I learned my worth, my true resilience, and the depth of our souls.

Lesson 5
Grief's Hidden Curriculum

Many in our culture have similar beliefs about grief—at least until we experience it ourselves. Generally, people think grieving is simply the sadness felt after someone dies. Many cite the familiar "five stages of grief"—denial, anger, bargaining, depression, and acceptance. But here's the truth: those stages were never intended to describe post-death grief. They were written for the terminally ill, and only three of those stages may actually apply to grief after a loved one dies. While denial can be a post-death grief expression initially, it is short-lived because you quickly realize your loved one's absence. Also bargaining has no place in the post death grief experience. The chips were down and the hand has already been played. There is no bargaining. Your loved one is gone. For the terminally ill bargaining is a last hope.

Most people who have not experienced loss believe the bereaved will be sad for maybe a few weeks or months and should then move on, picking up where life left off. But if you're reading this book, you know that couldn't be further from the truth. Grief has no particular expiration date. There are no steps or stages—just common experiences. While I don't believe grief can be neatly summed up in stages, it can be helpful to create a framework of possibilities to help you understand the struggle and ride its waves. One thing we can all agree on: grief is life-altering.

Here's my take. I call them the **Five Prospects**. I like the word "prospects" because it means the possibility or likelihood of some future event occurring. It leaves room for the variables of each circumstance and for the unknown and unexpected that the term "stages" does not. Here are my thoughts on what grief includes:

1. Shock: Numbness acts as a protection from the initial realization a death has occurred. It buffers the trauma violating your nervous system. You may feel disoriented, detached, and confused. Foggy brain, dissociation, and mental numbness are all common and actually a benefit to you for a time. It is a forced slowing by design so you can maximize your strength and allow your heart and mind to absorb the information of what has just taken place. Shock is not a bad thing. It can be the best thing for you initially. Without a shock reaction, the tearing away by death would be far more difficult to bear.

2. Detachment: Detachment from your old life can make the familiar feel unfamiliar. Your newfound feelings and emotions from heartache are uncharted territory. You can feel like an alien in your own body. Fear may set in. This can trigger physical reactions such as—crying, loss of appetite, insomnia, nausea, head, and body aches—and mental turmoil, including despair, longing, and endless looping thoughts. These become your new normal for what can be a very long while. Duration is different for everyone. The lesson you can learn over time is that you can have temporary times of relief when you accept the process and allow for good self care. It's not easy. Grief is hard. It's incremental. It's work.

3. Fight: Here comes anger. Anger at death itself, your loved one, God, yourself, or the world. This stage is pivotal—you can either get lost in anger and resentment or fight for your own well-being. Often the fight can feel like you're in a losing battle. Scrambling around trying to make sense of it all. Just when you feel like you have a sure foot, you get knocked down again and have to fight your way back. You're fighting to understand ***why*** and to find your place in this world again. It's pivotal because this is where you can make vast changes. Your fight increases your strength. You discover more about yourself and what you will and will not put up with or— you give in, give up, comply, pretend and allow yourself to take the blows. It's the space where decisions are made about yourself and for yourself. The fight is as many rounds as you give it, but your in the ring daily.

> **Note**: When searching for the answer to *why*—why did they die, why did this happen, why did they leave me, why did God take them—you may want to consider this: **If** you had the answer to that question, would it suddenly make you feel better? Take a moment to examine this question. If you knew *why* they died... would it ease your pain? No, it wouldn't. They would still be gone. The answer to "*why*" will not resolve your grief, but spending so much time asking that question in your fight, can stifle you. Why, why, why?

Instead of asking *why*, ask *how*. How do I continue my life without them? How do I get through today? How do I feel a continued connection to my loved one without their physical presence? Fighting for answers to *how* will support your healing, whereas questioning *why* can keep you trapped in devastation where no answer is good enough.

4. Perception: Your view of the world and everything in it has abruptly changed. Relationships, beliefs, priorities, and faith may transform. Life has a new interpretation, colored by the awareness of loss and mortality. Depending how you chose to progress, you can limit your perspective or expand your perspective. If grief is your teacher you will gain a perspective on life that cannot be gained by any other means. If grief is left only as your deep sorrow your view will be detrimentally skewed. This is what is meant by being on a grief journey. When you are on a journey you are in unfamiliar territory for discovery. Initially you may only have enough dim light to see the few steps in front of you. A mindfulness practice can be a great support for you here. You will perceive everything differently. It will be disappointing but it can also be a revelation into finding your true authentic self. Know that though the light may be dim now, possibilities await you down this road. Don't allow your deep sorrow to turn what little light you have off. Your eyes will adjust over time and your perspective will broaden and provide you with more light.

5. Connection: Beyond perception, you may find the soul of your loved one alive in memory and spirit. You strengthen the bond with them, yourself, your inner life, the world, God, and others. This is where grief can expand your heart, giving you experiences that transcend the pain. You may find a greater connection with your current relationships and, most importantly, with yourself. You can also unearth the mysteries of consciousness that is untouched by physical death. Your loved one is with you always just beyond the veil in a realm to be discovered by your willingness to find meaning to your deep sorrow. Grief is not for nothing, unless you give up the fight and close your eyes on your journey. Yes there will be days that will happen, but your connection can brighten the dim light and is calling you to see more.

The first three prospects describe experiences most who grieve are familiar with. Perception and connection, however, may be unexpected and full of twists that can change the direction of your life and put you on a path that was beyond your wildest dreams.

Perception and connection can begin even before the death has occurred and strengthen you to move through the post-death grief. This can happen most commonly when your loved one has a terminal illness and you have time to contemplate their passing.

Time Spent with Lori

One of my patients, Lori, was a 70-year-old woman who lived quite well and, by her own admission, had pretty much everything she wanted. She was an educator, a professor for the local university where she lived. She informed me that she had not thought much about spirituality for herself. She came from a family of educators, never attended any church, and was content with the life she had created for herself.

Now that she was facing her last days, she decided she wanted to prospect the idea of God, life after death, and mystical thought. She approached this endeavor intentionally and with calculation. Having been admitted to hospice she requested chaplain visits from her hospice team—not for comfort, but to test faith itself. I was a Spiritual Care Coordinator and was assigned to be her chaplain. When we met for the first time, she said, "I'll challenge you... are you up for it?"

I assured Lori that I was no scholar and not willing to battle theology, but I would happily engage in conversation about her questions and provide what insight I had based on my own experiences and study. She responded with, "I like you. Let's talk."

Over the following few weeks, we met and conversed a lot about her life, relationships, accomplishments, which were many, and also discussed, was her lack of "faith." Often our conversations ended in mutual acknowledgment: "We just can't know for sure." And that was enough for her to feel satisfied that she was not neglecting an aspect in life others seemed to care so much about.

One day, when I arrived, I witnessed that Lori's condition had deteriorated significantly from the week before. Her daughter informed me that she was barely taking in any substance and only small sips of water. She was very weak, and her face looked gaunt but at peace. Lori was fixated in a stare at the upper corner of her room when I walked in. I leaned in and asked softly, "What do you see?" Without shifting her gaze, she whispered, "God."

It is common in the dying process that the terminally ill have visitations from loved ones that have previously passed on. So I had assumed she would say a parent, spouse, or other familiar person that she had known in her life. This is the first time someone told me they were seeing *God*. Naturally I asked from my own curiosity, "What does God look like?" I expected her to describe a picture we have created for ourselves. Long robe, white beard, wearing sandals, sitting on a throne with a glow around this male image. Her simple but profound description was but one repeated word: **love… love.**

Lori, once a self-proclaimed atheist, was now experiencing a grander perspective and connection—one that could not be felt, explained, or debated in previous conversations. It was a sacred moment for sure. One that profoundly expanded our previous understanding about life and death. One that I will never forget. I understood that death was more than the limited view I had defined. And though I thought I had a pretty strong understanding of spirituality, I realized that there was so much more than I had been taught.

In hospice—and in my mom's final moments—I observed a consistent truth: death itself is often peaceful. The fear and suffering exist largely in anticipation. Most people, at the moment of death, experience comfort, sometimes through visions of departed loved ones, angels, or God. This truth has been significantly reassuring. Even when I have witnessed a painful physical decline, there is a moment as the soul leaves its host where acceptance, resolve, and peace come in that final breath. While we grieve intensely, our loved ones have reached peace. They are free from suffering, and we are left to try and make sense out of this transition. Changing our perception and connection.

It's not death we should fear—it's grief. Grief is the least honestly addressed tragedy upon the death of a loved one.

Let's consider other tragic world events: floods, hurricanes, riots, school shootings, and wars. When reported, focus is on the dead, memorials, and tributes—the lives that have been cut short. Certainly this is appropriate, but it's missing the larger toll. Rarely is thought given to the grief of the living. The effects of loss do not end in burial. In fact, the effects of loss proliferate. We must learn to address the suffering of the bereaved with time, attention, and understanding. And it is the community of grievers with grief as their teacher that is at the forefront of this charge.

In some other cultures where ones time of grief is honored, mourners are known in their communities and supported through the prospects of grief that they are thrust into. Jewish, Islamic, Greek Orthodox, Hindu, Mexican and Vietnamese cultures are some that provide structured support from family and community, caring for those who grieve. Many have up to a year, with the goal of witnessing stability. The burden and expectation of the bereaved are shared. Attention and respect is given, along with the freedom of the bereaved to express their grief openly.

Western culture has often embraced the stage theory: a linear progression toward recovery. But grief isn't linear. Variables are vast, and perception is cloudy. Life as you knew it is disrupted. What once felt secure may no longer be, and your worldview altered. The expectation of recovery falls on the bereaved alone after a very short time after the death. The support of family and friends simply fades away, and after weeks, avoidance of grief expressions sets in.

Grief, the Teacher, forces us to examine life in ways we never imagined. It highlights what is missing, which exposes our lack. It opens paths we didn't choose and challenges us to move forward, whether we like it or not. You cannot hide from grief. It will always return. Why? Because there is more for us to know—more than the cultural norms that we were raised to believe.

We are mostly alone with our grief teacher that we are reluctant to trust and view it as our affliction. The teacher engages almost every human life one way or another to get our attention. It causes you to undergo the duality of life, which provides the platform where the depths of love can fully be revealed. We will explore this in the next chapter.

Early grief alters cognition and perception. Focus, memory, and problem-solving may be impaired. Time may feel distorted. Emotional numbness protects you from overwhelming pain. Over time, however, you begin to question your identity and your place in the world. These are the questions that need to be asked and examined. The conversations that should be shared are too often hidden by societal platitudes and the progression of life itself.

However, grief makes you stand still—and if we are willing, we are able to see what we didn't know was there. The lessons that only grief can teach. Love never dies and is much grander than you could have ever imagined without your grief.

We often limit our perceptions to pain alone, but grief invites us to explore what is possible—like Lori did. Fear of the unknown may trap us, but grief, the teacher, paves a path into new awareness, expanding our emotions, thoughts, knowledge, and beliefs. It reveals a perspective once hidden, strengthening understanding and insight beyond what we once believed possible.

*There is more to this life than what meets the eye. What does **love** look like for you now that grief has opened it's door?*

Lesson 6
Required Coursework

Try to explain the word **up** without referencing **down.** Try to explain **in** without referencing **out.** Try to explain **on** without referencing **off.** Try to explain **light** without referencing **dark.** It's not so easy, is it? We learn these simple words very early in life and think nothing of it, because the experiences of up and down, in and out, and on and off are natural, common, and habitual. There cannot be the true existence of one without the other. This is the dichotomy of life: two sides are needed for one side to be fully understood.

While there are many theologies, philosophies, dogmas, and beliefs about why we live and die, why there is good and evil, and why suffering is part of our experience when we would rather live in bliss, the answer is as simple as the dichotomy of life. Knowing one requires knowing the other. The question I had to ask myself wasn't why the dichotomy exists, or why I should blame God—or a Higher Intelligence, or the lack thereof—for my suffering.

The question was: ***Knowing this dichotomy exists, why do I choose to stay in my suffering rather than find my way out?***

Grief, my Teacher, taught me how deep love can be realized through enduring the pain of grief. Not the love we casually say when hanging up a phone—*Love you, bye*—or the love we profess for a cheeseburger: *I love this burger*. This was a lesson in the essential meaning of life through the duality of how we suffer and how we love. A love that is unconditional and without question. A love that grows, reveals, and teaches. A love that has no measure, that sacrifices, that cannot be denied, and has no end. A love that grows even after death.

A few years after my divorce, I met, UN-purposefully, a man who was unexpectedly very kind to me. We quickly became friends, spending hours on the phone talking about anything and everything. I told him in no uncertain terms that I had no intention of ever marrying again. But he fell in love with a very vulnerable, broken, woman who appeared to be steady and strong. Honestly I kind of thought I was. I wasn't purposefully misleading him, I was just well practiced at knowing the right things to say, like I had my act together. Kind of like a method actor who aspires to complete emotional identification with the part they are playing. Again it was the only way I knew how to handle my trauma.

He has told me often, that he didn't love me for my looks, charm or wit. He said, **"I fell in love with you because you have miles and miles of heart"** which he has repeated often over our years together. My heart had indeed been shattered over and over again, yet I had a lifetime of experience pretending otherwise. That's not to say I wasn't kind or didn't have genuine love and compassion. I had learned many valuable lessons from grief about the value of each moment and kindness should prevail—but inside I was wounded. It was hard for me to see myself the way he saw me.

John is a big personality—from an authentically Sicilian family, raised in New York. He is generous to a fault, and his intentions are to do the right thing. His smile and open heart swept me off my feet. I had never been spoken to with such admiration. It was the first time I truly felt loved since my parents died. He gave me a safe space to be myself, feel my own feelings and examine who I had become by chance rather than intention. We were married within 18 months of meeting. It shocked my kids; I know they weren't prepared, and I know now that I brought some grief into their lives in doing so, which was never my intention. From my view, I believed they could only benefit from this new collaboration, not recognizing or considering the grief they too were denying. I thought I was being rescued from my despair. The grief of my family, my marriage, and the community my faith had provided me.

Life with John, my kids, my step kids, in-law kids and now my eight grandchildren has been fulfilling for me. I have been met with all kinds of dichotomies—good times, bad times; moments I embraced, and moments I wanted to run. All in all, I now recognize in myself that I have miles and miles of love for my family. The moments this unexpected partnership has fared won me a clearer picture of love. While we are far from picture-perfect and some struggles remain, I have an underlying peace that keeps me routinely steady, grateful, and aware of both the good and the difficult, finding new perspectives and growth in it all. I am living as intended, in the dichotomy of life that grief has taught me—not the despair that society would have me believe was my only option after so much trauma from deaths. I burned the banner hanging over me that said, *You Never Get Over Grief.*

I can't help but notice the difference in the kinds of love that Grief has taught me. I loved my parents. I felt safe with them and knew, without a shadow of doubt, that I was wanted and loved. They were kind souls. I have many wonderful memories with my extended family—Aunts, Uncles, Grandparents, and cousins. Family gatherings were fun, full of shared conversations, hugs, and some shenanigans. Love was apparent, shared, appreciated, and most importantly, never lost.

Over the years, as my family died—one by one—my love grew for them. It expanded, becoming deeper, more meaningful, and more cherished. This love is never uncertain or questioned in the grief experience. Grieving love never dies. It can't be stamped out, forgotten, or extinguished. It is alive, flourishing, and continues to express itself. That was unexpected. I've always loved my parents, but since their deaths decades ago, my love and admiration have only grown. So now my new banner is *You Never Get Over Love*.

This is hard for me to say regarding my disenfranchised grief of losing my marriage, family and friends who did not die but deeply hurt me and I grieved from the pain. The dichotomy of those losses is that they taught me what true love is. It wasn't what I thought while pretending everything was ok. Wishing I was deeply loved and cared about. Those relationships taught me to recognize true love when it came to me again. A love that doesn't disparage or betray. It stands strong in the midst of trial and uncertainty and prevails when all has failed. That grief taught me how to move forward to a purer form of love, like I had with my parents.

The things I remember about my parents lived on as I raised my own children. They don't even realize how much of their grandparents they experience through me. I made it a point to treat my kids with kindness and acceptance in a way that never allowed them to doubt how much I loved them and how wanted they are. I feel the same for my grandchildren. I try to be the grandmother I know my mom would have been if given more years—interactive, happy, and genuinely ecstatic each time she saw her grandchildren. Lots of love, but also lots of space to be themselves and embrace the dichotomy they are living.

Having lost my parents and knowing my kids and grandkids were robbed of ever knowing them prioritized my attentiveness and how I was going to ensure the love legacy of my parents would not end with me forever in deep sorrow.

Grief, the Teacher, has taught me to **love well.** To recognize the value of family and the time I have with them. Not to push or intrude, my love, on them in fear of losing them—a fear that they would die away, which was normalized in my early life. It's horrible to admit but I have imagined each one of their deaths in some sort of twisted way to prepare myself for the emotional breakdown I was sure to experience because it happened so often before. I had to address this fear often, and to this day I can be triggered into thoughts I thought I had overcome. Leaning in and moving forward through those triggers, I learned to give love space to grow naturally, with no expectation of return, satisfied in knowing that my love for my family will never die. **Never.**

I want to make a delicate distinction. Love in life is very different from love in death—and it is because of the dichotomy. For those of you who have experienced the death of a loved one, which I assume most of you have if you are reading this book, there is a distinct fact: your love has deepened into something grander than you ever felt while they were living. You may feel that you didn't express to them, strongly enough, how much you loved them based on what you feel now that they are gone. This is normal. It appears to be required coursework from the grief teacher.

When a loved one dies, you focus intently on that relationship. The highlights are brighter, and the challenges fade. You begin to idealize that relationship because of your longing and recognition that you will not see them again in this life. Your feelings for them intensify. As time goes on, you actively try to make some sense of your deepening love in their death which feels stronger than when they were alive. This is Grief the Teacher. Your deep sorrow magnifies what love is, its depth, magnitude, and infinity. Your love was always there but it was not fully realized until the subject of your love departed. This too is a dichotomy: when something dies, something grows. This truth is a universal principal.

We learn most about love and life through death. It seems cruel, but is it really?

I have longed for my loved ones to be present. I have missed them during milestones and defeats. I have wondered, speculated, and dreamed about what it would be like if they were still here. However, would I be the person I am now? Would I love my family the way I do now if I had not experienced these losses and the lessons of love that grief has taught me? Dare I ask—am I better off in my life because of my loss? That question alone makes me want to throw up. But I cannot deny that having gone through this suffering over many years, I now have a clearer vision to see the gratefulness, joy, love, and hope in life. It's the nature of the human experience that cannot be escaped. Can we learn to love as fervently without experiencing loss at all? I don't think so. Loss doesn't always come by death. Grief reveals itself through many types of loss as we have discussed. This is the great dichotomy. This answer alarms me. There must be a reconciliation between grief as the teacher of love. There's got to be more to it.

I will never be happy or feel blessed **because of** the deaths I have experienced; I would trade every grief lesson for another moment with my loved ones. That being said, I will also not live in the deep sorrow and depression that grief places at the door of its lessons. I have opened those doors, pressed in to understand life and its counterpart, death. I can now see more clearly the dichotomy of how grand love is because I have experienced the absence of those I've loved. This helps me in my current relationships. To not take for granted each moment of life we have.

The Grief Teacher taught me that death is only physical, but those I continue to love are eternal. We are connected in ways I would never have understood without this temporal time of separation from my loved ones. Yes, I said temporal.

I had to find out more. I had to make sense of this cruel dichotomy and question the stories that were preached to me to me about the finality of death. I had to explore my continued connection.

I had to ask the questions I was never allowed to ask.

Lesson 7
Head of the Class

I have had the rare privilege—although I used to think of it as a curse—of witnessing death multiple times, in multiple ways, and under multiple circumstances. Nothing has influenced my perspective on life like death. My encounters with it have dropped me to my knees and forced me to re-examine everything I have ever believed about dying. I could say I've seen it all and certainly more than most, but it is precisely because of my long and constant presence in the midst of death that I know there is still so much more to learn.

Caroline's Story
I was visiting a patient and her daughter who was her champion caregiver over the previous ten years of the patients life. Caroline her daughter was certainly more religious than I,

even though I was *her* spiritual care coordinator
and bereavement counselor. I remember visiting
her mother during the last few weeks of her life.
Walking into her home felt like entering a
sanctuary. Everything was meticulously
arranged, with constant hymns playing and a
large picture of *Jesus standing at a door* above
the fireplace. The Bible rested perfectly atop the
patient's chest. Her mother slept 20–22 hours a
day, only rousing enough to be cleaned or take
in a little nourishment. Caroline, was insistent
on providing her mother with the perfect death
experience. My role was to visit twice a week,
read from the list of favorite scriptures, and say
a prayer per Caroline's instructions.

I liked Caroline. She reminded me of a
Sunday school teacher I had as a child, a dear
friend of my mom's—no-nonsense, full of
boundaries, and unwavering in her adherence to
the Bible and church teachings. She towed the
line tightly. She was reliable and benevolent,
just as she had been taught. I understood
Caroline because, in many ways, years earlier, I
had been like her. Only I was pretending I had it
all together and I think Caroline truly did.

After her mother died—peacefully, in her
sleep, with hymns playing and Caroline holding
her hand—we continued to meet weekly.
Caroline was proud of the role she had played,
and her faith comforted her. She believed she
would be reunited with her mother in heaven, at
the feet of Jesus. This belief allowed her to move

through her tears quickly, justifying that there was no real reason to feel prolonged sadness. Our bereavement visits were her way of acknowledging her loss, and she felt 8 visits would do the trick.

On the third week after her mother's death, I arrived at Caroline's home and found her front door wide open. The windows were open, and the house was unusually quiet—no hymns playing. I knocked several times, calling out, "Caroline... hello... Are you there?" Moments later, she came running to the door. "Thank God you're here," she said. "I don't know how I'm going to tell you this. You won't believe what's happened. You're going to think I've gone mad. I'm a mess."

I walked inside and noticed her house was no longer immaculate. Dirty dishes filled the sink, unfolded clothes were on a chair, and a blanket and pillow were left on the couch— evidence she had slept there. The refrigerator contents covered the counters and table, and Caroline herself looked disheveled: her hair was loose, her clothes wrinkled, and she appeared exhausted. My first thought— grief has taken hold of her sensibility.

It occurred to me that her grief reactions had been delayed and she was now feeling the full throttle of sorrow. Caroline had lived a highly structured life. She had been dictating how she should grieve rather than allowing grief to dictate to her. But I also knew grief—the teacher never gives up. There is only one winner... grief. You will feel your loss, whether you recognize it or not. Caroline was shaken to her core, and I was about to witness just how transformative this grief lesson would be.

Instead of her usual warm welcome with a drink offering with a cookie or muffin, Caroline was frantic, pacing, and barely coherent. She repeated, "You're going to think I'm nuts." I gently took her hands and said, "There is nothing you could say that would make me think less of you, Caroline. Let's just sit down, take some deep breaths. I'm in no hurry. I'm here for you."

Moving the blanket over, we sat down together on the couch. Caroline grabbed the half empty glass of water that appeared to have been sitting there for some time. Unlike herself, she guzzled it down and wiped her mouth with her forearm. She squared her shoulders with me and said, "You're not going to believe what I'm about to tell you."

Caroline began by describing her routine since her mother's death and how she had managed well until two nights ago. That night, she became restless and couldn't sleep. She tried music, reading the Bible, and praying for everyone on her list—but nothing worked. Her mind wandered to thoughts of her mother: *How is she? What is heaven like? Did she get a nice place past the pearly gates on Golden Street*

Lane? Does she get to cook again, like she loved to do?

Finally, after a couple of hours of wrestling in bed, she decided to make herself warm milk, as her mother had done for her as a child. She flipped on the lights as she made her way to the kitchen, where she grabbed a glass from the top cupboard and a small saucepan from the bottom. Opening the refrigerator, she saw the bulb inside flash a couple of times when the most bizarre, unexpected sight startled her.

Caroline saw her mother's floating head inside the refrigerator.

Caroline yelped, slammed the door, and stepped back. Taking a couple of deep breaths, she chuckled at herself, reasoning that she was more tired than she thought. Rubbing her eyes, she tried again. Once more, the lights flashed, and she saw the holographic image of her mother's head smiling at her. Stunned and trying to make sense of what she thought she was seeing, she stepped back and rubbed her eyes again and again. Then her smiling mother spoke five words:

"It's not what you think." Within moments, the image faded.

Caroline shut the door and ran back to bed. She instinctively thought she should be alarmed, but instead she felt oddly at peace and fell asleep. The next morning, she naturally thought it was all just a dream. She returned to the kitchen, where she found the lights on. The glass and saucepan were exactly where she had left them in her so-called dream. Reluctantly Caroline opened the refrigerator but there was no image. She took everything out of the refrigerator to see if she could find any reason for this unexplainable occurrence. With nothing out of the ordinary found Caroline spent the day praying, struggling to reconcile what had happened and what her mother's message meant.

That next night, Caroline decided to throw all common sense away. She made a bed for herself on the couch and kept the refrigerator open, disregarding the food that was spoiling from being left on her table. She fell asleep quickly from being so tired from the night before. Half way through the night she awoke with thoughts of her dear departed mother. She quickly looked at the refrigerator and the door had been closed. So she got up, opened the door and once again she saw the flashing light and her mother's smiling head repeating, "It's not what you think," before fading away.

Looking for my expert advice, Caroline asked me, "What does this mean?" In true counselor fashion I replied, "What do you think it means?" because clearly I didn't have a clue. I was leaning towards agreeing with her previous statements that she did in fact go a little nuts, but her conviction of the event was astoundingly real, at least to her. I didn't want to discredit the strong, logical Christian woman I knew. Over the next few months, we discussed her experience, focusing not on whether it was "real" but on how it made her *feel.*

In my work, I've witnessed many spiritual experiences, but none like this. When people describe their mystical phenomena I always ask: do you feel afraid, or comforted? Like most, Caroline's answer was the same: comforted.

Those five words—*It's not what you think*—have stayed with me. Death is not what we think. I was taught that there was life after death but absolutely no communication until you were reunited by dying yourself. When the body ceases: breath stops, heartbeat stops, brain stops, and the soul enters a tunnel to the light. It's far away and unreachable. Caroline agreed with this theory until her undeniable experience that begged to question, if it's not what I think, than what *is* it like to die?

My Experience With Death to this Point
Weeks to months before death: a person becomes fatigued, their appetite decreases, sleep time increases. Priorities are reduced. What seemed so important to them before, hobbies, responsibilities and routines lose their value. Fixation on end of life preparations take

precedence along with communicating their affection to people they love.

Weeks to days before death: withdrawal from others including previous interests and even family begins. No appetite and little intake is common as the digestive system begins to shut down. Increased sleeping, possible agitation unlike their normal character, seeing and speaking to deceased loved ones or angels as though they are standing in front of them are expected. I call this—*one foot in, one foot out*. They are here and they are also there.

Days to hours before death: some may possibly get a brief energy surge. Then breathing becomes labored with shallow respiration, and the sound known as the "death rattle," which is just secretions that have built up in the throat due to the inability to swallow. This is far more difficult on the care giver than the patient. What is not often known or talked about is that most people wait until everyone leaves the room before dying. I believe this is because they are aware of your grief and it is too difficult to leave in front of you. I didn't leave my moms room when she died, but she did wait until we had all drifted off asleep.

Unlike what is depicted in the movies, less than 1% of people that I have witnessed die, speak a meaningful last word shortly before their last breath. It's just not likely given the state of their current physical condition and should never be expected. The essence of who they are is already in motion and transitioning to another realm. Their physical body is simply shutting down all its circuits.

When you are able to purposely witness a last breath, where the death is not sudden or you are simply not giving attention to it, you can feel within your own soul that something is lifting from the room. I'm not sure how else to explain it. You know that they have left their body and transitioned. Concurrently you also know that they have left with you a piece of their essence. It feels like an expanded presence is with you. Similar to having your eyes closed and you can sense when someone is nearby. If you are close in relationship with the deceased, your grief draws them even closer. It is a unique spiritual connection that can only be felt, better than described.

Not being personally related to the deceased, the experience is still meaningful. You can feel the presence lifting but it quickly fades because the grief isn't there in the same way as it is for those in relationship. Grief is parallel to the nature of the relationship and the continued connection is parallel to your grief.

If a basic stranger like me, as a hospice representative, can be profoundly impressed by the spirit of someone transitioning, it seems reasonable that there is more to the story than an abrupt final ending. Words do not do the experience justice. You kind of need to be there, but no one really wants to. Another dichotomy.

Should we reframe our beliefs about death? The phrase—*I lost my loved one*—is misleading. They are not lost at all. If anything our beliefs about death and grief causes *us* to be lost, but our loved ones are not lost. They have simply been released from the tethers of a physical world. Physical death is final, but your relationship has transitioned and continues. Caroline's mother's words—*"It's not what you think"*—reminded Caroline that spiritual connection persists beyond physical death. Her rigid beliefs gave way, allowing her to experience peace, love, and hope beyond earthly limitations and restrictive traditions. Grief got her attention and taught her a lesson about love that only it can teach.

It's not what you think. There's more.

Lesson 8
Class Rules Don't Apply

When we say the words *life after death*, we most often refer to our belief in heaven—or, perhaps, the idea of people going to heaven or hell. Everyone has questioned this for themselves. Is there life after death? Many scientists often deny it, while spiritual leaders preach it. The question itself is really more about our consciousness than the place. We wonder about ourselves after death. Does someone's spirit, soul, personality, essence survive physical death? And if so, what will it be like? Do we have a soul? Do we live forever in heaven as we are? Do we take on an angelic form or does the soul return to earth, reincarnated? Is there the possibility of eternal damnation? When we die, does our consciousness die with us, leaving us unaware of who we are? Or is this all there is—

life on earth, then death, over and out? Game over. Poof. Gone.

Based on all the evidence across tens of thousands of years, we still cannot provide a single answer to that question that will satisfy **all** of humanity. We all just want one simple, fundamental answer to a question that plagues us all at some point. So what does that tell you? It tells me that Caroline's mother's floating head was right: *it's not what you think.* You may have a wonderful philosophy, belief, theory, idea, plan, or guess, but this simple question will never be easily boxed up with a perfect bow. The evidence, experiences, knowledge, and uncertainty are far too vast for a simple patented answer.

While this can sound disconcerting—or even alarming for those strongly convinced of *one truth* or another—consider the positive side of **not** having a definable answer: *wonder.* Openness. Possibility. I do have a viewpoint that I am fairly confident in, and it provides me personal satisfaction while I meander through my life. But the fact that there are multiple possibilities keeps me assuming and inquisitive. All I have to go on is my own experience from my unique journey. And if my experiences have taught me anything, it is this: what we maintain as "*truth*" is merely one possibility from our singular perspective. What I believe may be utter nonsense to others because their journey is completely different.

With that being said, I do want to explain my humble opinion. For me, it is far more difficult to prove that life and consciousness end at physical death than to believe in life after death. In fact, there is zero evidence that there is no life after death—because if there were nothing after death, there is nothing to prove *nothingness*. By that deduction, I cannot buy into the ideology that consciousness ends entirely. Those comforted by the idea that there is no life after death often appear uncomfortable with life itself. The mere thought of there being something more is daunting, and not having assured answers, a singular truth, brings uncertainty. For them, the idea of no life after death offers hope that the suffering they endure in life will finally end. I am in no way judging anyone for this school of thought; in fact, I understand it.

I have spent countless hours with hundreds of people struggling to reconcile earthly suffering with the possibility of a continuum of consciousness. Yet the evidence for continued consciousness is overwhelming for me—too overwhelming to consider there is nothing after death. On the flipside my encounter with thousands of death experiences forced me to be a witness to the *it's not what you think* theory. Truly one size does not fit all.

Multiple Encounters
In the hospice I worked for, the expectation was at least 21 visits per week. Factoring vacation days, overtime, weekends on call, and so on, I easily averaged over a thousand visits per year with the terminally ill, their families, and the bereaved. I worked in the field for 22 years. You do the math. My time spent with dying, death, and grief is well above average. The stories I have witnessed, the life stories shared with me, and my own personal encounters with dying, death, and grief allow me to speak with some proficiency. So one might think I have all the answers. The truth is, I have more questions than answers.

I entered my career with a fairly strong belief system—only to have it challenged in every way. Eventually, I realized that if my beliefs about life, death, the afterlife, and consciousness were worth anything, I would have to let go of every single belief I had once clung to. Every... single... one. If it was true, it would stand the test. If there were flaws, I trusted that deeper truth would reveal itself. My goal was peace of mind. I examined my life, my existence, my spirituality, my soul, my faith, my relationships and how I derived my thoughts about them. I researched other philosophies, ideologies, faiths, spiritual practices, and sciences. I explored history, sociology, and culture. I listened to and read accounts of near-death experiences, and of course, I had countless spiritual encounters while working in hospice. I witnessed hundreds of deaths, walking the journey alongside terminally ill patients. People are incredibly honest about their fears and beliefs when they know their days are numbered. And still, the answers I found are bigger and grander than any of us can fully comprehend. We need each other to even begin to understand the questions that extends beyond our physical life.

A Point of View I Never Imagined
I was once called to attend a death by one of my RN colleagues. She had been at the home of a male patient everyone called Papa. He was actively dying, lying in a hospital bed in the living room, comatose with mouth drop, spiking fever and labored breathing. There were 30–40 grief stricken family members present, anticipating his last words that would never come before his final breath. The RN said, "I'm not trained to deal with all this emotion. Please help." I arrived within 30 minutes. One panicked family member had already called 911 without the RN's knowledge, to resuscitate Papa—who had not yet stopped breathing.

In hospice care, resuscitation is not appropriate for a terminally ill patient who has a signed Do Not Resuscitate (DNR) order. Resuscitation is not effective on a patient who's vital organs have mostly shut down. It is a violent action, and the patient must already have no pulse and not breathing for the emergency treatment to begin. On the off chance it succeeded, the patient would be left on life support, forcing the family to make the choice to turn off the machine as a terminal ill patient would still be terminally ill with organ failure. Resuscitation is for persons who have a chance of full recovery. Resuscitation was not part of Papa's plan and would not have the results the family longed for.

When the paramedics arrived they informed the family there was nothing they could do as the patient was still alive. While the nurse monitored the patient, I focused on managing the families emotional state. I asked each person to share their favorite stories about Papa, which seemed comforting. This activity did in fact calm the temperature of the room.

Soon after our share time, a family member watched as the nurse positioned her stethoscope looking for Papa's pulse. The RN softly announced, "I'm sorry, he's gone." Silence fell—like the hush before a newborn's cry. As expected came a loud outcry of reality pouring from Mrs. Papa who collapsed onto her husband's body, screaming, "No, no you can't be gone!" and demanding he be checked again. Her daughter in agreement shouted, "Call 911!" I thought I succeeded in stopping that call. She walked away from me and dialed without delay to save her father.

Thankfully, the RN convinced the wife that the patient did in fact die and resuscitation was not an option. Upon this realization, she fainted. By the time the paramedics arrived for the second time, the RN had treated Mrs. Papa and got her comfortably to her recliner with some juice to sip on. The paramedics explained once again that they would not be able to successfully resuscitate the patient and it would be against his predetermined wishes.

As the paramedics were leaving the RN quickly gathered her belongings and followed suit. Our hospice program's policy was that someone from our team would stay with the family until the mortuary arrived to pick up the deceased. It was determined by the RN that the someone would be me.

Chaos is too light of a word to describe the next three hours. The Body Removal Attendants were delayed due to the time being after hours on a weekend and their GPS guiding them to the wrong house. Can you imagine the surprised looks on those folks' faces when they answered their door to the unexpected body removal guests. Meanwhile two of Papa's daughters decided to have what I accurately would describe as an emotional display and others would call a pissing match titled— *Who Loved Papa More.* Wailing, crying and flailing around the house as if they had no control and raising the bar when the attention of annoyed family members swayed to the other. The youngest daughter won as she fell to the floor, having witnessed earlier what a fainting spell looked like, attempting to convince her audience that she also fainted. Sadly she was not a good actress and yet someone called 911 for a third time. I wasn't aware of the call until my old friends, the paramedics pulled up in front of the home and only one person got off the truck to see if this was another false alarm... which it was.

This young responder informed the family that they were abusing emergency resources and they should not call again as charges would be brought for their inappropriate actions. As I walked out to the truck thanking and apologizing for their arrival, they pitifully wished me luck and left me once again alone with the emotional wreckage from grief.

Trying my best to find a way to manage this situation I encouraged the family to clear the area around the patient and allow each person who desired to take a few minutes with Papa and say their final goodbyes. This common ritual by many families and cultures takes place before the body is removed. One by one the family lined up and paid their respects. Kissing his cheek, patting his hand and leaving tears on his chest as they hugged him goodbye.

As time passed, the crowd had grown, as the present family was informing extended family of the news and reported they would arrive soon. It appeared that the worst of the emotional outbreaks were over— or so I thought. Every area of the house was full with standing room only. You could smell the aroma of food as the Aunties were busy in the kitchen preparing a feast. Suddenly, without warning someone screamed, "Oh my god... it's a scorpion!" Instantly this controlled environment failed.

Women screaming on their tip toes and the men jumped into hunt mode yelling, "catch it, catch it" — while coming up with strategies for its capture. I admit, I did feel the immediate reaction to jump onto the chair next to me. I have seen the pain of a scorpion sting and I would do anything to avoid it. Playing it cool, I stood there like a statue, praying silently that the scorpion would not take notice.

One of the young men only a yard away from me informed, "There it is... kill it, kill it!" — then Mrs. Papa broke away from her grief and bellowed, "STOP!" which hastened an immediate response of silence from all. Through tears of recognition she exclaimed,

"It's Papa... he was a Scorpio."

My confidence in my own ability to manage highly stressed situations of the bereaved was devoured that day by the sheer feeling of insanity. I wondered, *why was I here, in this moment, with these people, doing this for a job.* The young hunters did in fact catch Papa the scorpion and they decided to cage him and put him in the garden where Papa loved to spend a lot of his time when he was— a human being. A strange but sweet sentiment to Papa —this man they so dearly loved.

The mortuary did eventually arrive. Everyone kindly said their goodbyes to me shortly after Papa's former body was driven away in the mortuary van. The once feared scorpion actually brought a sense of peace to this family that I never could have achieved with compassion, words of comfort and assurances. Oddly enough I showed up for work the next day, as if the day before was just another typical day at work.

The Grand Perspective

This experience taught me nothing concrete about the afterlife—but it does demonstrate that if we open ourselves to possibilities, anything is truly possible. Did I believe the scorpion was Papa? No. But for that family, believing it offered hope and a sense of connection—to him and to each other. Comforting words, laughter and sweet memories were being exchanged and love was deepening for Papa and each other.

My Christian upbringing had once disallowed me from connecting with deceased loved ones. It was considered morbid, even satanic. Yet my own experiences proved otherwise. I felt the presence of my parents, guidance, comfort, and love. I witnessed countless families having similar experiences:

visitations, messages, and signs that defied
rational explanation. Over time, I realized that
connecting with loved ones begins not with
mediums or psychedelics, but with trusting
yourself. Believing in the grander perspective
beyond what is observable.

We do this every day. We believe in air we
cannot see, gravity we cannot feel, and
technology allowing us to reach someone
around the world in a way most of us cannot
explain, yet it works.

Grief is the teacher of a grander perspective.
Grief creates the opportunity, desire, and belief
we need to connect with those we love who have
transitioned. Grief rips apart our old selves,
leaving us students of life, death, and the
continuum of the soul. It teaches that there is
not one perspective—there are many. What
works as truth for one may not be truth for
another—and that is okay. Grief teaches
diversity and inclusivity because it is powered by
love. Physical life has a beginning and an end.
Finding meaning in the in-between matters to
the after life. And this great marvel *love* should
be the common thread, allowing us to heal and
find hope throughout our grief journey.

These are the conversations that society
unknowingly longs to hear. An acceptance
beyond our self inflicted boundaries. To be kind,
open and loving when we don't agree or even
understand each other. Grief reminds us that
our time here is short in a way that can feel long

at times. We as a species are in it together whether we like it or not. You know, perhaps Papa orchestrated that scorpions visit to send his message of love. True or not, it worked.

Making a way for differences also makes a way for understanding through the common ground of grief.

Lesson 9
Accelerated Courses

Dying.
Die.
Death.

These words strike an uncomfortable chord in
each of us. They can dredge up frightening
images and ignite deeply rooted feelings of
tragedy and fear. For those who have not
experienced the harsh blow of a loved one who
has passed, often work hard to ignore these
topics and avoid them at all costs. Death
conversations can be considered taboo—morbid
to discuss—even among those who are dying.

In my experience, some families will
absolutely refuse to discuss the inevitable. They
will stand together at death's door. The evidence
is all around, yet they choose to avoid, pretend

and look the other way, just as my family did, because death feels like the worst possible outcome. So intimate words don't get exchanged. People don't say what needs to be said, and do what needs to be done, even though they know—deep down—that their efforts to avoid the inevitable will not succeed.

We have been taught our entire lives to fear and hate death. Did you or your parents shudder at the simplest of losses, like when a child's beloved hamster died? You know the story: *How will you ever tell your four-year-old? Should we just go to the store and replace it so they never find out?* If we struggle that much with a hamster, how are we expected to handle the death of a grandparent?

There is an unspoken expectation that children and grandchildren will outlive their grandparents—right? Yet while death may be anticipated in old age, it is certainly not limited to it. I used to tell my hospice patients, *You could outlive me.* There is always the possibility that I won't make it home today. Grim words? Yes. Possible? Also yes. Sadly, many of you reading this have experienced the shock of an untimely, unexpected death of someone you deeply loved.

Oddly enough, children are often the most resilient when it comes to accepting death—and I mean true resilience, not faux. The younger they are, the more naturally accepting they tend to be. They are not weighted by the discomforting beliefs about death that adults are. Children take their cues from the adults around them. Some adults avoid the discussion entirely and put on a brave face. Again my parents' preference. Others sob openly, isolate themselves, or display devastation without restraint. Adults respond to death based on how they were *taught* or what they may have witnessed.

While many parents worry about how their children are grieving, they would often be wiser to pay attention to their own responses. The watchful, trusting, learning eyes of their children are absorbing information. The opinions will be formed through their observance. So the question should be asked; *What do you want your children to learn about the probable tragedies and grief they will undoubtedly encounter in their lifetime?*

Because death and dying were prominent themes in my young life—unlike those of my friends—it is something I have thought about often. My early experiences taught me to fear death and its residual effects. I have spent too much time carrying the burden of fear that those I love may die before I see them again. I was strongly opposed to my children playing with toy guns or watching violence, no matter how cartoonish—like Wile E. Coyote being blown to bits while chasing the Road Runner.

Those early lessons about death left triggers that I still try to dodge to this day. They often show up as worry, ruminating thoughts of getting an unwanted phone call and the grief that follows. This particular fear was my shadow. Whenever they left the house, my mind flooded with images of them not coming home. "Be safe," I would habitually say, while imagining every possible disaster. It wasn't just a casual phrase for me—it was a desperate prayer inspired by multiple family deaths.

Worry became my constant companion hiding behind an easy going smile: fearing something that had not happened, with odds slim to none. Even now, I consciously choose different words—*Have a good time, see you soon or stay safe*—because they shift my focus from fear to hopeful expectation. I don't want to miss the joy of each day by fixating on the worst that could happen.

Is that denial—or is it mindful living instead of wasteful worry?

What if having a healthier view of death with intentional thoughts, could change how we live? Could it reduce fear and make room for joy? We have to look at this—don't we?

What if we were taught to see dying, death, and grief through a broader lens? Stay with me here. I am not suggesting we put on rose-colored glasses or deny the reality that someone we love is here one moment and gone the next. We miss their tangible presence deeply—of course we do. But what if we viewed death from an eternal perspective?

What if conversations about dying weren't defused, but instead were the most intimate, soulful, and connective conversations we will ever have? What if we were taught that while the physical body dies, the soul—or consciousness—does not? That our physical relationships turn to *transitioned relationships*. A term I'm examining more fully.

After witnessing countless deaths, I can come to no other conclusion. This belief is not unusual. According to the Pew Research Center, globally, more than 70% of people believe in some form of life after death. While those beliefs vary, the core idea remains: life continues beyond physical death.

This belief is supported not only by religion or faith traditions, but by countless documented experiences: near-death accounts across cultures describing profound peace; reports of consciousness during periods of brain inactivity; out-of-body experiences with verifiable details; children recalling past-life memories later confirmed. It seems there is overwhelming evidence of continued consciousness.

End of Life Conversations

One of my patients was a beautiful 42-year-old woman named Maureen. She had dark brown hair, dark brown eyes, and a welcoming presence. I met her in her mother's home, bedridden in a back room, ravaged by colon cancer that had metastasized throughout her body. When I entered the room, she was coughing and spitting up. Her mother who had guided me to meet her, quickly grabbed the basin and washcloth from the over-the-bed table and placed it under her chin – an action that instantly triggered memories of my own mother's illness. Despite her discomfort, Maureen, gestured for me to sit. Normally, I would have stepped out to provide privacy, but she didn't seem to mind—so I stayed.

Maureen had three young children, all still in elementary school, now living with their father whom she had divorced years earlier. Due to her physical decline Maureen chose to stay with her mother so her children would not have to witness the daily deterioration of her body. With tears streaming down her face, she said, "Leaving them is the hardest thing I have ever had to do."

Maureen had fought for her life the previous four years with everything she had- but now her body was entering its final stages. She knew her life was coming to an end and there wasn't a damn thing she could do about it.

We connected immediately, as if we were old friends. I loved her right away, and I cherished our visits. Though I typically saw patients weekly or biweekly, Maureen asked me to visit daily. "You'll get sick of me," I joked.

"I'm already sick," she replied with a grin. "Please come every day—if you can."

So I did... every day... weekends included. She lived for three and a half months. Cancer doesn't take a day off—so neither did I. Visiting Maureen didn't feel like work -it was an honor.

Much of our time together centered on her children. Maureen wanted to leave them personal remembrances of her. We recorded her reading their favorite stories, she wrote letters and created photo albums. She would laugh and cry at the same time reminiscing through her memories. We talked about what she wanted to say to them on her anticipated last visit. "I'm not going to lie" she said, "I have to tell them the truth." Those conversations were among the hardest—and most sacred-I've ever had.

I encouraged her to see herself as their guardian angel, to give them permission to talk to her when she's gone and feel her continued love and guidance in their heart.

This was the conversation I wish I would have had as a child. How comforting it would have been to know my mother was just a thought away—that our connection hadn't ended, only changed. That she was eternally connected to me -a valuable relationship that could not be severed by physical death. Consciousness, personality, memory, love— these do not disappear. Once again I must implore the body dies, but the relationship transitions.

As Maureen declined, she grew weaker and more afraid. She slept most of the day and barely sipped water. As I held her hand she would whisper, "Please pray for me. I'm so afraid."

My faith had evolved a lot through hospice work. Where once I relied on tidy answers and religious platitudes, I learned those words often failed the dying. Standing so close on this side of the veil to eternity, knowing you would not meet in this time space reality again, the message you want to convey should resonant. I sensed that much of what I had been taught about life, death, and God was incomplete. I knew—deep in my soul—that there was more.

Maureen told me, "You need to write a book about prayer. You say what I want to say, but don't know how." Truthfully, I was terrified of saying the wrong thing. So I prayed from the deepest place of presence and connection I could muster —and poured my heart out from her point of suffering, to the best of my ability. This too was a lesson for me. My own grief rose to the occasion to meet Maureen's in a manner that tied our souls together in deep sorrow, deep understanding and a deep kinship.

Twelve days before her death, fear increased as her body declined. She would fight to stay awake fearing she wouldn't wake up again. "You're not dying today Maureen." I told her with some trepidation that I may be wrong. But my spirit told me otherwise. "You know you will die when you receive a peace in your heart and your mind. You will know when you are ready." I incited.

I had witnessed this phenomenon before with other patients. A peace that passes all understanding enters the heart and mind of a patient not long before they pass.

On my next visit, I expected continued decline, but when I arrived her mother said joyfully, "Wait until you see her." Maureen had just received a bed bath. Home Health Aids are the true angels of hospice work. "I feel like I was taken into the shower, scrubbed and cleaned." She gushed, "Smell me. I smell so good." Delight and relief filled her eyes. She was experiencing a burst of energy. This is a possibility for the dying. We giggled and joked as she described her new found comfort amongst her decaying body. Quickly her mood turned solemn.

"Kat" summoning my full attention, "I got it – I finally feel at peace. You are the only one I can tell."

She talked about tasting food again and getting out of her god forsaken bed. It was a short conversation -but the content of each statement felt like a novel. Our previous visits and open dialogue had created a space where she could say everything she needed to say.

Sadly, it was to me and not her dearly loved mom who couldn't bear the strain of grief and always left the room despite Maureen's consistent invitation.

Two days later, she slipped into a coma and died peacefully.

This story has a lot of meaning for me, but unfortunately no one wants to hear it. The details are lost because it's too sad or too depressing. If only we were taught that death is a natural part of life and while there is sorrow, it is also a story of love, overcoming fear and being freed from suffering. How friendships can be made in the rarest of circumstances with little time left. I made a dear friend in Maureen and she died. I am grateful for even the short time we spent together. I still feel a sense of her presence, her warm smile, sense of humor and her encouragement to finish this book. I feel her approval to changing its topic from pleading prayers to validating the emotions of the death experience and learning from the accompanying grief.

Acknowledged or not— I am confident that you feel the presence of your loved ones too.

Grief, the teacher, reminds us that death is not the end of love. Grief invites us to expand our understanding, to see beyond the physical,

and to recognize that connection does not end—
it evolves. While the topic of death can be
difficult, the dichotomy offers a look into love
that should be discovered and more importantly
discussed. Why do we continue to hide from
pain? Why do we find ways to numb ourselves
and avoid a path that starts dark but can be
illuminating? With lessons that can strengthen
our entire existence so we can emerge from
suffering endlessly.

I have stood in line at a grocery store, sat at
a park picnic table and waited in the sitting area
for my name to be called at a restaurant — and
strangers have approached me, with their
personal story about the death of their loved
one. The grief coach vibe must be oddly
apparent to those who are grieving around me.
Truthfully it bothers me sometimes because I
resort back to the long held cultural creed of the
western society that these discussion should not
be had. It feels against the grain even for me in
such random scenarios. However, if grief could
come out of the closet we've shoved it in, we
may be able to eliminate unnecessary fears
about it.

*I see the good that can come from transparent
grief, but I'm haunted by habits of long
held misinformation.*

Lesson 10
Teacher Got My Attention

Sometimes the smallest flippant remarks can challenge you in ways you never imagined. Every part of your grief journey holds keys to unlock the misinformation that you once held onto so tightly and provide you with evidence that will expand your mind and spirit that can change your trajectory. It is a great bravery to walk through your grief with an open heart and mind.

A Haunting Story
I had a patient once whose formal name I shared, Kathleen, that lived out in the middle of the desert and was, in no uncertain terms, a hoarder. I had seen messy yards plenty of times before. They are relatively commonplace in the desert, where homes are often built on large lots

in the middle of nowhere. Honestly, what does one do with a broken tractor? Apparently, no one knows for sure, so they let them rust on their property and pile other unwanted things around them. But Kathleen's home was the first—of many—hoarder houses I would eventually visit.

As best as I could tell, when you walked through the front door, you were in the living room, which opened into a small dining area, with the kitchen off to the right side. If I had to guess, the piles were about five feet high. I am 5'8" and could see over the tops of what looked like a cornfield maze. To this day, I would say it was the most organized-looking hoarder house I had ever seen. There was roughly an eighteen-inch-wide path that wound through the piles in a serpentine pattern, like the waiting line at an airport.

I heard a rough female voice yell, "Over here. Make your way back here. I've got a chair for you." Sure enough, I eventually found my way to a four-by-five-foot clearing with two chairs, an end table, and an oxygen tank. Thank God the oxygen was turned off, because Kathleen was puffing away on a cigarette, which still felt alarming to me, due to the countless piles of old newspaper and magazines, She appeared to be conscious of the danger as she kept an ashtray on her lap and flicked the loose ash often.

In my career I've known a few cases where patients did not heed the warning of smoking around an oxygen tank— which led to increased suffering and in some cases an early demise.

This was clearly not the safest environment, but it was home to Kathleen, and she seemed perfectly content with her way of living. She never apologized for it, and we never discussed the obvious. My job was not to judge—it was to listen. That mandate has served me well. Looking past the obvious in life helps us see the gems.

Kathleen mostly wanted someone to talk to. Her adult son lived with her and came and went throughout the day. She had a twenty-inch box television perched atop one of the piles—God only knows where it was plugged in. What she truly enjoyed, though, was conversation. She was funny, full of stories about her childhood and her *good-for-nothing husband who left her for a floozy.*

We visited weekly for several weeks until I told her I would be taking a two-week vacation. I offered to have a volunteer come by for a chat while I was gone, but she declined. "You better come to see me when you get back," she said. I agreed.

Then she added, "If I die before you get back, I'm coming to haunt you—and don't think I won't."

Honestly, I wasn't quite sure how to process that, so I just replied, "Sounds good," and carefully unwound myself back out the door. Wouldn't you know it—Kathleen died suddenly when her aneurysm burst, one week into my vacation.

I was raised with a firm understanding: there were no such things as ghosts. Angels and demons—yes, ghosts—no. Talking about connecting with the dead was strictly forbidden. There was a deep taboo around spirits, mediums, tarot readings, séances, Ouija boards, ghosts, goblins, and yes—even Halloween. My Auntie Jo died on Halloween, which only solidified a decades-long hatred of the holiday. I don't watch scary movies. I don't go to haunted houses, even for fun. I made my children dress up as biblical characters or cute animals and took them to church harvest festivals instead of trick-or-treating like the other kids in the neighborhood. Honestly, I didn't care for Halloween alternatives either.

A Little Spooked

To say I had a phobia about spiritual connections after death would be an understatement. I'm a little embarrassed to admit all of this, but it's the truth. I carried so much unexamined fear around death—teachings about the devil, hell, damnation, and the evil spirits—that I prided myself on rising above it all as a woman of faith. I believed I was doing the right thing by refusing to participate in what I saw as such a dark holiday as Halloween.

To be fair to myself, when I was about twelve, I had a strange and frightening encounter that left a lasting imprint. A very young woman came to our church with her two-year-old son. I babysat him in the nursery down the hall from the pastor's office while the pastor and deacons counseled her and arranged safe housing. As I understood it at the time, she had been involved in Satan worship. Her parents were leaders in a Satanic occult—or so I gathered from listening to the adults whisper about it.

The story I heard was that she had been raised to be a "breeder." I didn't fully understand what that meant until later, when I learned it involved giving birth to children without government records—no birth certificates, no identification. When the child turned two, on Halloween, they were to be sacrificed in a ritual. Her son had just turned two, and she was trying to save his life.

I never learned how that story ended. I was too young to verify any fact or to ask any questions. But the fear it planted in me as a young child was powerful. It came with an unspoken rule: *this belief must never be questioned.* Even now, when I examine my belief system—how it formed and whether it holds truth—I can still feel the tug of that warning... whispering; *Don't question this belief to stay away from all things about hauntings, ghosts and talking to the dead.* It was strong. It was formative.

Sorting Through It All

Grief, however, is not a liar. It is organic, raw, and relentlessly truth-seeking. That is why I believe grief is not merely a reaction to loss, but a teacher—one that chased me like a hungry wolf. Loss after loss, grief met me at every turn. Even the grief of that young woman and her child stayed with me. The grief of lost jobs, homes, pets, divorce, family, friends and beliefs I had inherited—all of it demanded something from me. Grief wanted truth, and I am still working through the details as misunderstandings reveal themselves.

Although I often felt led into silence about spirituality, I was never unaware that there was more—so much more—to consciousness, soul, God, Source, the universe, angels, and the possibility of connection after death. I grew up Pentecostal, a very evangelical, turn-or-burn environment emphasizing the baptism and gifts of the Holy Spirit. There was a sharp distinction between good and evil, and stepping out of line felt like risking my eternal destiny.

In the seventies, during my teenage years, there seemed to be endless debate between: hippies, Jesus people, Catholics, old denominations, non-denominational churches with no spiritual gifts, and non-denominational churches with them. How does one keep up with all the competing "*one truths*"? At the time, I mostly loved that drums and guitars were allowed in church and that songs didn't sound like dirges.

I share all this so you can see that I was caught in the swirl of a spiritual tornado. Sure, I learned the language for each setting, but what was happening in my soul was something else entirely. I already knew when God—Holy Spirit, Source, the Universe—was speaking to me and through me. It didn't care what name I used. I moved away from masculine pronouns for God long before it became common, because the divine, in my experience, isn't so easily boxed in. Giving God a gender limited my view of an infinite creator.

I knew when my mother, my father, and other loved ones were present and guiding me. I wrote back and forth with them endlessly in journals—and then burned the pages, so my conversation with the non-living would never be revealed. Occasionally, I'd share something my mom had "said" to me, framing it as a joke, just to see if anyone would admit they did the same. Such as, "Oh well, my mom says you did it and she can see everything." No one ever alluded to hearing from their dead loved ones. So clearly I couldn't share openly.

I experienced what Pentecostals would call *words of knowledge*. I knew things about people—what they were emotionally carrying, worrying about, or seeking guidance on. Not word-for-word thoughts, but deep concerns. Sometimes I would approach them and say, "I don't know if this means anything to you, but I think I got a word from God for you." I was never wrong. Tears often followed. Relief always did. Still, I held back, afraid of crossing some invisible boundary built by those I trusted more than myself.

After my divorce, I stopped going to church for many reasons, one being that I felt closer to God on my own terms than I ever did within church walls. I'm not against church; I am against the idea that attendance alone equals spiritual growth. Even Jesus advised going from home to home, and he openly criticized the pretenses of temple leaders. Ironically, hospice work mirrored that model of home to home for me—meeting people where they were.

I often confessed to family and coworkers that I hated my hospice job. It challenged every belief I had, and I didn't want to be challenged. I wanted an easy job—something simple, like grocery clerking— where the biggest problem of the day in my mind would be someone's squished bread. I was exhausted by death talk and uncomfortable with the questions it forced me to face. Every belief I had developed to that point seemed as though it was being called into question. I had done such a good job, bottling things up tightly and pretending through the contradictions of my faith vs my experience. Kathleen's comment about haunting me cracked open a door I desperately wanted to keep closed.

Grief wouldn't let me retreat. It was easier to stay inside my Christian bubble, armed with platitudes like *God knows best* or *He won't give you more than you can handle*—which, by the way, isn't even in the Bible. (The scripture states and I paraphrase; God won't *tempt* you beyond what you can handle. I Corinthians 10:13.) Those answers don't satisfy someone with ALS, tongue cancer, or an open chest wound crawling with maggots. No wonder hospice hires chaplains. The terminal world dismantles tidy theology. I found this to be true when calling churches to visit their members who were now on hospice. Many pastors simply would not visit their dying members. The few who did, and I mean few were of the elite in my perspective.

This is grief—deep sorrow, devastating circumstances, blasting noise and spitting truth in your face. Grief clings until you either surrender to despair or open yourself to possibility. It teaches that life is brutal and breathtakingly precious. Lonely and communal. Death, when faced honestly, becomes an invitation rather than an ending.

I never felt haunted by Kathleen. I refuse to associate her death with darkness or that her statement to me was anything other than a loving joke hoping to see me again. We had no idea at the time how her comment would shed so much light to my weak viewpoint birthed in fear of the dark. Kathleen lived for years in the residue of pain. I believe she longed for light and created pathways for it. Her humor paved the way. I was reluctant to enter her world and aware of the risks. I wish I could say I came purely from compassion, but sometimes I came because I needed the paycheck. Still, the light in her heart met the light in mine, and together we softened the darkness.

It took ten long, battle-worn years of hospice work for me to stop running from being haunted by my own grief. I remember the moment clearly—sitting alone in my midnight-blue Honda Civic in the office parking lot, furious that my life revolved around dying. I could see the value of my work, but I was drowning in discomfort. Crying out to a faith that felt poisoned by the subjective beliefs of others who delivered its message.

God and belief in God are not the same thing. One is love, intelligence, consciousness, source, wisdom, joy, and non-judgmental presence. The other is merely what we think about it. I know you can have a belief in God and know nothing about the magnitude of this presence.

Finally, I gave up. I threw up my hands and said to whomever was listening on the other side, "I'm done. I can't fit into this box anymore. I don't believe in anything the way I've been taught." Not through the fault of the messengers but through my own lack of responsibility to question, understand and know what I believe. I pleaded, "Reveal your spirit to me on your terms and not mine." Grief brought me on this journey to discover there is more— *it is not what I think.*

Even though my old fears screamed blasphemy, my conviction to seek surged.
And grief—the teacher I never wanted—was finally getting my full attention.

When you open yourself to spirit and the possibilities that this life is just a small portion of what is to be discovered you can not only find a knowing that those who have died are rooting for you, loving you, and guiding you – you find a peace that is indescribable. The loneliness disappears and longing changes to finding time to commune with your inner guidance. You acquire a greater compassion for yourself. You begin to understand the path you are on.

You begin to see a future you never thought could be possible since the day you buried your loved one.

Lesson 11
My Favorite Subject

It has taken me many years of letting go of the old and allowing the unexamined in. I began my exploration into what was previously disallowed by trying to meditate. I had heard it was good for the mind, body, and spirit—and Lord knows I needed all of that.

My belief was that meditation was more of a Buddhist thing. Sitting in a lotus position, fingers in the "OK" position (or so I thought at the time), resting on your knees and saying *OMMMMM*. Meditation was never taught or encouraged by my church or any spiritual teacher I knew. This left me to believe it was wrong and against my religion—despite the fact that meditation is taught and encouraged throughout the Bible.

Breaking Open

I had been taught, not by my parents but by influencers in the church that Buddhists were bad—that Buddhism was a cult worshiping a big, fat-bellied statue. Looking back, it became clear to me that I needed to do my own research rather than trusting those who most likely never researched the subject at all.

I started reading about Buddhism, which led me to other religions and belief systems and their histories. I had always loved learning about ecclesiology—the study of how Christian churches began—so this felt like an expanded version of that curiosity. I couldn't get enough. I had read about many doctrines in the past and already knew the basics of several belief systems through my hospice families.

Learning about Buddhism became my quiet rebellion—the unleashing of buried curiosity.

The Vietnamese Zen Master Thích Nhất Hạnh spoke about how Buddhism isn't a religion but a practice. He was instrumental in bringing mindfulness to Western culture. The Buddha statue, I learned, isn't worshiped—it's symbolic, much like the cross for Christians, the Star of David for Jews, or the Kaaba for Muslims.

While I had no interest in becoming a Buddhist, it was the *relational* part between God and humanity that interested me. Oneness with self and the God consciousness within. Just like Jesus said the kingdom of God is within in you. Oneness with God, meditation and mindfulness is approved in some form across nearly all religions. It felt like a good place to begin my connection to God... a god... *the* God... *some* God. I loved the inclusivity of it.

I was no spring chicken when I started meditating. Sitting in a lotus position wasn't just impossible—it was another box in belief. And I was fairly certain that instead of experiencing *namaste*, I would end up *nama-stuck*.

So I tried sitting quietly and comfortably wherever I was until I felt inspired to do something else. That was my meditation. Usually within two or three minutes, I was up again—my mind racing through my mental to-do list like a hamster on a wheel. I later learned that these were ruminating thoughts which are natural. I briefly wondered if thinking about *doing what needed to be done* could count as meditation. You know, maybe with the right attitude? No. If that were true, most of us would be master meditators. I realized I had simply jumped back into my usual box of stress and productivity.

I didn't want to read too much about the practice because I didn't want to be led by just another person telling me what to believe. I was looking for my own path. If that path brought information to me I would read it but I didn't go on my usual research hunt. I decided—on my own—that meditation meant clearing my mind of all thought. So I practiced clearing my mind while driving home from work. (Not my smartest idea.)

I would glance at the clock in my car, think of nothing, and wait. As soon as a thought appeared—as it naturally would—I'd look back at the clock to see how much time had passed. It was always the same time on the clock when I looked again, meaning only a few seconds had gone by. I even tried pulling over to the side of the road only to have the same results. I could clear my mind for only a few seconds at a time. Honestly I never got higher than 7 seconds.

Clearly, I needed Instruction

One day I happened upon an interview with **Michael Singer**, author of ***The Untethered Soul***. I loved the title immediately. The interview played in the background as I multitasked. Much of what he said resonated with me and some I had no idea what he was talking about, but I heard enough to know I needed that book. It wasn't a long book, but it took me forever to read. Each chapter held so much insight—ideas I had never explored, yet somehow already knew.

It was as though I had been asleep and the book awakened me to a grander perspective that I knew existed but couldn't see because my learned beliefs blurred my vision. Much of my religious teachings became clearer to me while others did not hold up. Many didn't even stand up to the actual core teachings of Jesus.

The book wasn't about grief, but I bought several copies and gave them to hospice clients who were searching for meaning. They, too, sensed there was more—yet struggled to release traditional definitions of grief and loss. I knew I had been led to that book. It expanded my view, like rounding a bend in the road and suddenly seeing farther than before.

I learned that meditation wasn't about posture, hand positions, music, or even eliminating thoughts. Meditation was about being present—and releasing thoughts as they arise without opinion or judgment. When a thought appears, you notice it and let it go. You don't engage it. You don't argue with it. You simply notice it and release it. You observe.

If you become distracted, and you will, simply move yourself once again into the quiet present moment. You are not a failure, you don't have to start over- you are experiencing normal habits that with regular practice will change. You will become more relaxed and long for more time to sit in the peace you will come to know.

With time and attention to breathing, the mind softens. Thoughts slow. It's a rest for the mind, body, and spirit—a pause from the relentless rat race.

I finally understood why it's called a practice. *You never complete it. You always practice.*

I often read and heard from others— to begin, *find* a quiet time for yourself. I never had quiet time for myself. I was incapable of "finding" quiet time, so I changed the word from *find* to *create*. And suddenly, I had time. Especially in the beginning of your practice you do not need an hour set aside. Even three to five minutes can make a difference. Uninterrupted time is what matters. Finding a comfortable position. Closing your eyes to minimize the distraction. Take a deep breath in and exhale and your there.

I would find a few minutes, several times a day. That's how it began for me. Once I began it became harder to stop. I enjoyed these little moments of solitude, that it took me away from the unrelenting, ruminating thoughts and allowed me to see a clearer picture of every circumstance rather than the stressed version I had been living in. Breathing techniques, focus points or guided meditations are all wonderful but not necessary. Soon my few minutes turned into my entire lunch break and craving time to meditate. I stuck with it. I didn't judge it- I just practiced.

I practiced constantly. I taught patients and families to find relief from the pain and mental weight they carry through their crises by offering this simple and profound practice. Not all bought into it and some with little effort decided that they are not capable of it because of the way they are built. I never pushed. If you believe you can't than you can't.

Onward, I learned how the brain never truly shuts off—but we can choose which thoughts we follow. We can choose to stay with our thoughts or we can choose to let it go. After meditating I often feel content, at peace, inspired, having an awakened perspective and a deeper connection to something greater than myself. To God or the term I prefer to use now is *Source*. For me the term God triggered old held beliefs and put me back into a system of traditional thought created by others. I was committed to my own discovery and *Source* feels more accurate to my connection.

Source often led me back to scriptures I had known but apparently never fully understood even though I thought I did: *Be still and know.*
Take every thought captive.
You will keep him in perfect peace whose mind stays on you.

The more I studied different belief systems and opened my thoughts to receive deeper guidance from Source, for me personally, the more I could see the underlying core message of it all: **love**, connection. creation. God reveals not Himself to us—but *ourselves* within creation.

Grief and suffering has a dualistic path. It is through grief and our feeling of deep loss that we truly have the opportunity to learn that there is so much more to the life we have been living, the relationships we have, and the power we have within ourselves to participate in the energy that connects us to all. The grieving mind is introduced to expanding thought and revelation beyond what has been normally comfortable to discuss.

My ability to console those who were traumatized by their grief grew. I taught those who were willing, to allow their grief to teach them.

Tears are reminders of great love.
Longing helps us open to unexpected
connections.
Sadness reminds us how precious good times
are and not taking advantage of the
opportunities to know joy.

If we don't allow grief to teach us the lessons of life and love then these following words are appropriate- you truly have a loss, you will never get over grief and death is final.

It was decades before I allowed myself to see beyond my pain. I could look back with regret but mindfulness shows me that if I do – I lose my present. My mindfulness and meditation practices became my normal. I began *automatic writing* long before I knew it had a name. I would sit quietly, clear my thoughts, and type or write whatever came into my head. Like mindfulness, without judgment or opinion. The thoughts are always inspiring. I believe them to be messages from a higher collective intelligence that we all have access too, with willingness and trust. Some may call it God, others Holy Spirit, others the Universe, others Ancestors or those who crossed the veil before us. Names and titles are not important. What is important is the connection and the guidance provided, best revealed by our teacher grief.

I finally allowed myself to talk to loved ones who had passed, or as I prefer to say transitioned—and to listen. Often there were no words, only a sense of love, gratitude, and presence. Where I once discouraged such connection in the bubble of beliefs where I resided , I now see this communication as natural. Clients often say- "I know this seems weird but I find myself talking to them." I now respond, "There is something weird if you don't."

My Personal Connection

I listened to an interview with an American psychic/medium, author and television personality. He shared that he did not want his abilities as a psychic/medium initially, because of the stigma and his own personal skepticism he had against psychics in general. He told a story about his own experience attempting to connect with his mother who had passed away. He asked for a sign with great doubt and then forgot about it. He wanted to prove his ability to connect as faulty. Weeks later with all doubts

erased he received the sign he asked for in a
remarkable way he would have never expected.

Interestingly enough, most credible psychic
mediums educate that no one needs a psychic or
a medium, nor do they need to be psychic to
connect with the other side. It is something we
are all capable of.

I decided regardless if I believed him or not,
this sounds like fun. With great whimsy and jest
I asked my mother for a sign: specifically a
hibiscus flower. Pink and white hibiscus were
my mom's favorite flowers and we had 3 very
large bushes that lined the house in our side
yard, so in my mind this would be a meaningful
sign. I didn't care what form it came, a word, a
picture, the actual flower. I was even open to
different colors. I wrote it down with a date as
proof of my request.

At first I looked for a hibiscus everywhere.
Being a tropical flower it was unlikely to see one
in the high desert where I live, which I knew
when I chose it. After a week I gave up figuring
it wouldn't work for me. What is true for one is
not necessarily true for another. I never told a
soul, knowing it sounded ridiculous. And frankly
I just didn't care that much about it. It's also
true that if I put to much hope into receiving a
sign I knew the opportunity for disappointment
was great.

Three weeks later, my 10-year-old
granddaughter Skylar—who never met my
mother, nor did her dad, my son —asked me if I

knew what her favorite flower was. This was the
start of a guessing game we often played
together. She asks the questions and I guess. I
threw out the typical choices- daisy, rose,
sunflower, tulip. "Nope, it's a hibiscus!", she
said with glee and proceeded to show me a
photo of the exact type my mother loved. Pink
and white. Then she showed me pictures of a
hibiscus necklace, earrings and T-shirt she
wanted— random, unsolicited.

*This wasn't a coincidence. This was a
connection. I felt the immediate joy of my mom.*

Oddly, the next day my step son and his wife
came to visit from Florida. Sitting around the
dining table chatting away, I told them about the
hibiscus connection with my mom. Ryan and
Ashley looked at each other. Then Ryan
proceeded to show me a picture of a hibiscus
bush that he had texted to Ashley the day before
asking if she wanted it for their yard.
What seemed completely unlikely was now
confirmed and brought me a great sense of joy
and wonder. My sweet mama made herself
known from beyond my understanding.
Would I know this connection could exist
without grief? Would I understand the
magnitude of the soul without loss? Would I feel
my mother's present love over four decades after
her death without being open to what is

possible? Grief the Teacher became the dearest of friends.

I get how unnerving this can be for those of us who have been tethered to our old belief systems. At times my old self peeks it's head and I feel like– a heretic, but that feeling is always surpassed by the feeling of wholeness. The missing pieces are falling into place and my soul is expanding. I am grateful for my religious background. It gave me hope, and a framework in which to ask the most powerful questions – who am I? Why am I here? Is there a God? Whatever your framework is I'm not asking you to abandon your beliefs or to change what you believe now – only to have the willingness to believe there is *more*.

*Grief grants a perspective that religion may deny. We do not exist to live in limitation but to experience what seems impossible. There is more. From an eternal perspective,
there is always more.*

Lesson 12
Hard Classes

Grieving is like a hard-boiled egg: fragile on the outside and hard on the inside. If you don't address the needs of the hard-boiled egg and leave it unattended, it begins to stink—and no one wants to be around it. Have you noticed people you used to feel close to, backing away? This can happen for many reasons. Your circumstances may trigger grief in them or awaken their fear of death. There are often unexamined beliefs at play. Perhaps, dare I say, your unattended grief has left you stinky—hard to be around. Perhaps the qualities that once made you delightful now feel dark, and you cannot see life past the loss of your loved one. You are trapped in a box of sorrow, and you neither can nor want to find your way out.

One of the hardest parts of my job as a grief counselor wasn't sitting with the bereaved, listening to their tears and pain, or feeling the tugs of my own grief while supporting another. The hardest part was trying to help someone who refused to be helped. Sadly, in my experience, that was the majority of people I met. It didn't matter what I said or did, or which techniques I offered—they chose their misery over any glimmer of hope. They were grieving as they had been taught- *I will forever grieve my loved one and that means only sorrow and suffering.*

I wholeheartedly admit, without hesitation, that grief is by far the most difficult challenge one can face. I also wholeheartedly admit that no one knows the depth of your pain as you do— even if the type of loss is the same or you are grieving the same person. Grief is one of the most shared, yet uniquely individualized, challenges we will ever experience. When someone says, "I know how you feel," they don't. They can never know exactly how you feel. But that truth should not be a weapon you use against yourself to hide in a box of sorrow. Your pain, loss, fear, shame, and depression are not permanent fixtures unless you allow them to be. You can choose to learn from this awful robbing of your soul—and become, dare I say... better.

Many bereaved people do not believe they can recover from grief. It is repeated, promoted, and accepted that you will never get over your loss, that you will always grieve, and that no one fully recovers. I agree with these statements with one caveat: if you believe you will never recover, you won't. If you believe you will always grieve, you will. Belief shapes your experience. What a sad state we create when we write the tragic ending to our loved one's story like this:

My husband and I had a great life together—then he died. Because of that, I chose to grieve deeply and gave up all hope that life had anything left for me. Even on rare good days, instead of embracing joy and imagining my husband happy for me, I allowed a dark cloud of sorrow to hover over every event with the thought: He should have been here to see this. I could never allow myself to feel true happiness because he is not here with me.

While we can blame a society that fails to support the grieving, in meaningful ways, it is ultimately up to us to find our way. To break out of the self misery box—yes, self inflicted misery—and see the bigger picture of what has happened. Initially our grief is deep sorrow but over time we have practiced our pain so well it becomes a self imposed misery box.

Our sorrow is fragile. If we do not nurture it, it hardens into feeling sorry for ourselves. We shut others out, cease to invest in new or current relationships, and forget that hope for life still exists.

Our shell is fragile and inside we are hardened.

I could tell hundreds of stories about people trapped in this box, their hearts hardened, reciting over and over that recovery from grief is impossible. They often seek sympathy, entangling themselves in a web of victimhood that multiplies their sorrow—and often manifests in chronic illness, anxiety disorders, depression or even worse disease.

Some readers may find my words harsh, thinking I lack sympathy or understanding. The opposite is true: I understand all too well. I choose not to sugarcoat grief for those who cling to it. Yes, grief is long, painful, and unavoidable. Yes, this devastation will pierce your heart in ways rendering you unrecognizable. Yes, grief will be triggered repeatedly throughout your life. Yes, there are often no words sufficient to express this pain.

I am not minimizing your grief and I'm not denying grief's impact. I am denying that you must surrender the rest of your life to it.

One Women's Quick Sand

Consider Claudia, one example among many. The first time I met her, she refused to let me in. She was too upset to speak to anyone and asked me to leave. I left my contact information and said, "No problem, but please call me to reschedule." Claudia's husband had died three months earlier.

A week before this first meeting, her son called, desperate. His mother refused to leave the house, accept help, or allow support. She cried constantly and declared her life over. Neighbors and children helped with groceries, mail, bills, and cleaning. Claudia still dressed, bathed, and fed herself, and her son believed she was too strong a Catholic to consider suicide—though she often said, "I wish God would take me now."

Claudia had four children and several grandchildren, all left by the wayside in her grief. She had been a loving, devoted mother and grandmother, active in family life. Her husband's death marked the end of her participation, as she retreated entirely. Her family had to bury their dad but they also had the combined tragedy of losing their mother, not to physical death but to the hardening of her heart. She succumbed to the grief and loss.

The next time I went to Claudia's, she invited me into her living room. She informed me that this meeting was her son's demand and she had no strength left to fight him on it. Clearly she had no intention of participating in grief counseling and was letting me know the best way she knew how.

Across from me was her husband's recliner, transformed into a shrine: a folded lap blanket, framed photograph, his flannel shirt draped over the chair, slippers neatly placed in front. Several other belongings were thoughtfully adorning the arms of the chair. Her devotion was undeniable. Her efforts to honor him in this way were symbolic of her adoration.

I am in favor of having an area in your home for pictures, candles and personal items while working through your grieving process. However, at some point, chances are, you will need to take it down. This process can be daunting, similar to cleaning out your beloved's closet, but more difficult because a shrine or memorial becomes somewhat sacred. The emotion it took to create it can feel like you're being ripped apart when it needs to be moved or taken down for any reason. I recommend that home memorials remain small and easily transported. They should be reminders of joyful memories and provide comfort not sorrow. If it's a picture, an item and a candle it can be easily moved and placed with more convenience than if it's a large area left untouched.

For Claudia her memorial was a desperate attempt to cling onto him. She told me that she tries to forget he has died and pretends he is still sitting there with his favorite things.

Claudia informed me that I would not be able to help her. Her husband had been taken from her and there is no going back. She cried the majority of the time throughout her declarations of loss and barely let me say a word. Thirty minutes passed and she stood up and told me it was time for me to go. I thanked her for allowing me to be present at this difficult time and politely requested to come back the following week. Reluctantly she agreed.

Over six 30 minute weekly visits, I listened to her same story each time without challenge. I knew it was the only way I stood a chance to gain her trust. On the sixth visit, I asked, "If your husband could speak to you now, what would he say?" She looked at me with surprise and began to cry, replying, "He would be mad at me." When I asked why, she said, "Because I have chosen to give up on my life until I die."

Claudia knew the choice she had made. She believed in her heart that she must sacrifice the rest of her life and any possible joy she may have to somehow prove how much she loved her husband. I tried to point out that she was not only sacrificing her own happiness but continued relationships with her family. She understood the cost of her decision—not only to herself, but to her children and grandchildren. Yet she remained unwilling to accept help. At this point there was no value in our continued visits. I am incapable of helping those who are not willing to receive. I checked in with her son monthly for over a year. Last I heard her kids and grandkids visited rarely and the family they once cherished fell apart.

Claudia's effort to show her undying love actually buried the legacy of love her husband had sewn.

Sadly, this scenario is common. While there are varying degrees of this story it is important to understand that we who grieve need to promote the discussion that recovery is possible. Recovery is not equivalent to forgetting in any way. Grief can be immobilizing, but recovery is possible. To recover is to regain a state of health, mind, and strength—to reclaim something lost...yourself. Recovery is not only possible, it can expand your life in unimaginable ways and it validates the depths of your love story.

What is it that may be holding you back from recovery? For me it was avoidance of the pain. I looked like I had recovered, but it wasn't until I allowed the teachings of grief to show me its duality that I began to engage in the vitality of life. I'm not the same person as I was before grief, and now I don't want to be.

For you it may be similar to Claudia. Pain and suffering feels like the only connection you still have with the one you love. You may be thinking: *If I stop crying or feel time of happiness then I'm leaving my loved one behind.* How could that be true? This belief begs examination.

Another Perspective

Let's switch roles. What if I had died and my mom was alive. What would my hope be for her as she continued on without me. While the death of a child is unimaginable, even in the midst of experiencing it – the child with all his

or her hopeful joys would never expect their
parent to stop being the wonderful caring,
nurturing person they knew.

I would expect my mom to be the kind,
warm, witty caring person she had always been
to me. The essence of who my mom is should
continue to advance, to grow and love more. Of
course the physical process of grief is inevitable,
but the physical part of us should not devour our
soul. Our soul should guide our physical mind
and body into recovery.

For you – what would your hope be for your
loved one if it was you who had die?. Would you
want them to give up their future happiness? Of
course not. That seems so unreasonable from
this point of you. So now, I will ask you the same
thing that I asked Claudia. If your loved one
could speak to you now – and I believe they can;
What would they say? What do they want you to
know? What do they hope for you?

*Are you willing to honor their wishes for you?
In doing so, is that not the best memorial you
can give to them?*

Grief the teacher, when listened to, asks us
to look at these questions and answer them
honestly. These are the questions from a loving
relationship that has not died. Grief encourages
us to learn that the soul, the spirit, the essence
and energy lives on in you. Relationships are
more than physical. If you only have a physical

relationship with someone then it is fleeting. Relationships are soul to soul, spirit to spirit, essence to essence and a constant exchange of energy.

Most of us are blessed with more than just one relationship. Those relationships also need to be fostered and can deepen because of the lessons of life and love from our grief teacher. As we recover from our grief, we also solidify, strengthen and empower the love of our deceased loved one and the love of those we still share this physical time with.

Through my own grief, I have learned to live fully, love more deeply, value time and set better priorities. Darkness highlights the light in my life; sorrow illuminates joy. When grief has fully taught us, we no longer take love for granted. Recovery is possible. Life can continue—and even move you in directions of your newfound desires. Your loved one is not lost. They are present, guiding, supporting, and loving you still. That is only if, you don't lose yourself in your grief process.

A Story of Recovery

A couple of months after her husband passed away Pam contacted me for grief support. She had been married to her husband for over 3 decades and she described their relationship as soul mates, best friends, one of a kind and not typical. They met in their late 30's and instantly fell in love and were married 2 months later.

With no children they were each other's companions, traveling frequently, and enjoying the spoils life afforded them.

Pam could not remember a day in her marriage where they were not together, chatting, holding hands and retiring to the same bed each night. They chose to never be apart. They lived fully in the present and never once discussed the day that death would separate them.

But it did separate them. Tom had quickly become very ill. Residual affects from his time in the military during the Viet Nam War. His breathing was erratic and he would have episodes of passing out. The doctor's had some difficulty diagnosing him but soon agreed that he was suffering from Mesothelioma. According to the CDC, the Mayo Clinic and the American Cancer Society, mesothelioma is a rare aggressive form of cancer that develops in the thin lining (mesothelium) of organs, most commonly the lungs or abdomen. It is primarily caused by asbestos exposure and has a long latency period of 20-30 years before symptoms begin to appear. It's incurable and the treatments are solely focused on managing the symptoms.

Pam described the countless doctor's appointments, tests, misinformation and devastation when Tom's diagnosis was finally confirmed. They refused to look at death still. Fighting everyday for life until they were turned away from the hospital and forced to sign up with hospice. Tom died two days later. Pam said, it still felt unexpected and sudden. She couldn't even look at the death of her husband until it was looking at her.

With no local family and very few friends, Pam stayed in bed for weeks. She would get up long enough to clean herself and get something to eat, mostly ordered in and go back to bed. She couldn't bear to sit in her family room where she and Tom shared their evenings together side by side. She closed the door of his home office where Tom spent most of his day and informed me at our first visit she still hadn't opened that door.

Pam and I met weekly and I learned that she and her husband were agnostic. They never discussed heaven, the afterlife, and kept focused on the present moment. She told me it felt like discussing anything about death would be a bad omen and the invitation to inviting problems. So they never did, even in Tom's last days. "Looking back" Pam shared, "I can see that Tom tried to tell me things that I wouldn't listen to. He tried to tell me he was leaving but I just couldn't – I just wouldn't… and now I can't have that conversation."

I ask the question of Pam that I have asked of you. "What would he say now?" Pam smiled and said, "I know exactly what he'd say. Can I talk about that? I was afraid you would think I was out of my mind."

Pam told me that when she allows herself to think about her husband, she talks to him and she can feel his loving response to her. She thought she may be imagining it, but claimed she didn't care because it was the only time she felt relief from her pain. She longs for the tangible Tom but she is satisfied by the spiritual, soulful connection she had. I validated Pam's experience and encouraged her to move forward with her impressions.

Where many might discourage this, for the fear that the bereaved will stay lost in a relationship with a dead person, I disagree. Validating this phenomena allows the bereaved to move away from the sorrow and into discovery, which is by far better to work through, finding the possibilities of a transitioned relationship with your loved one rather than the ruin left by depressive grief.

The year anniversary of Tom's death was approaching and Pam had since worked through the struggles of cleaning out Tom's office, making dinner for herself and sitting alone in the evening in their family room to watch a movie or read a book. She shed a lot of tears coming to terms with missing the touch of his hand and the warmth of his smile. She found comfort knowing he was present with her at every moment. She could feel his continued love and approval of her choices to do something good for herself.

She decided she would take a trip that she and Tom had often talked about but never went. On the anniversary of his death she took in the breathtaking views of Saint-Tropez in Southern France. She felt the bitter sweet moment of wishing Tom was there and knowing Tom was there with her in spirit, seeing the same view from another space in reality, with only a thin veil between them.

Pam was not the same person she was before Tom died. But as she put's it, "I'm unlimited now. The worst thing that could happen did and it couldn't break our love."

In the years to come, Pam found another man to love. A widower who understood Pam's journey. Together with the felt approval from their first partners, they shared their stories, and began to feel a new love brewing. This love would never, could never replace the love Pam continues to have with Tom. But there is room for it all.

Grief teaches us that love is unlimited. Through desperation we cling to unexamined knowledge and resist considering alternative thoughts. In time by our allowance and breaking the limitations we've bound our love with, we learn that love is so unique to each relationship we have. It is impossible to be replicated, nor does it need to be – because it's eternal. A living energy that cannot be extinguished by a physical death. Why wouldn't we want to experience more?

For some the thought of beginning a new relationship is unbearable. The thought of having any relationship can be unthinkable. Like Claudia you may have chosen to be a martyr to your grief.

I encourage you to take the risk from what you have known and allow even a glimmer of light into the deep pit of sorrow – lifting you to the challenges of recovery and a grand perspective unforeseen.

Lesson 13
Lesson Review

For review, I want to take a moment to reflect on what we've explored. These lessons have been about more than grief, more than love, more than life's challenges—they've been about the lessons hidden in the corners of our experiences, the truths that quietly wait until we are ready to see them.

We began with the understanding that our lives have many shifting experiences. These shifts in life cannot be avoided. They are often called milestones, celebrations or on the opposite side - traumas and tragedies. Either good shifts or bad there are always choices within those shifts that can lead us to something better, something worse or avoidance all together. What is consistent is that we have a *choice* to how we are going to respond. Some shifts cause non-negotiable changes in your behavior that protect and enhance your future. Others can blind you and set you on an unnecessary path that is heavier and longer than the initial blow.

Knowing this and giving self-care and deserved attention to ourselves, we learn that through it all, love shines its light, always present, always showing you a way, regardless of how dark your journey. Leaning into your grief, paying attention to your needs, opening to possibilities and finding honest support, no matter how difficult, will prove to be the better route.

We also learned about flowing through the movement of your grief instead of resisting it. When you fight against every emotion, every expression, every feeling, every change, you are denying the grief you are in. You are setting yourself up for more suffering, physical unrest, and possibly more personal loss. When you allow yourself to let go of your resistance, you make space for learning more about yourself than at any other time in your life. You are not letting go of your loved one – you are letting go of the devastation between you. You can make room for a clearer understanding about your transitioned relationship with them, and the continuum of the love you share.

While riding this crazy roller coaster of grief, your life powers on in multiple aspects and there is no getting off. The Grief Teacher is there to show you how to ride. Let go of resistance, allow space for your expressions and be open to a world with a grander perspective where you can know the presence of your loved ones spirit and the comfort they bring.

In the Accelerated Course on Love lesson we learned— that love isn't always easy, neat, or convenient. Sharing our grief experiences and pushing through the discomfort of difficult conversations can forge new territory undiscovered and unavailable except by the common ground of grief. We need to ask the question of ourselves are we willing to break new ground and open the door for others who are grieving. Creating time and opportunity for conversations we are afraid to have that lead to self discovery.

We explored the teacher in every situation, the ways grief, loss, and life's challenges can demand our attention and open our hearts. The stories of Maureen, Kathleen, Claudia, Pam, and others were not just anecdotes—they were mirrors, showing us that every sorrow carries a lesson, every loss holds the potential for growth, and every moment of despair is a doorway to discovery. Grief is not a punishment; it is a guide. It teaches us that life is fragile, precious, and meant to be experienced fully, even in the darkness.

We learned that connection is eternal. Whether through meditation, conversation with Source, or the gentle signs of our loved ones who have transitioned, the bonds we share cannot be broken by death. They shift, they transform, and they expand. We discovered that our spirits can reach beyond the tangible and touch what feels impossible, and that the universe has ways of answering even our quietest prayers.

We looked at awareness and presence. Meditation, mindfulness, and opening ourselves to the possibilities beyond our conditioned beliefs are not about achieving perfection—they are about showing up, noticing, and letting life speak to us. Every breath, every pause, every moment of reflection is an opportunity to step out of the box we've been taught to inhabit, and into the vast space of awareness, love, and understanding.

And perhaps the most important lesson of all: life continues, even after profound loss. We can recover—not by forgetting, not by moving on in a way that diminishes our love or our grief, but by moving forward in a way that honors both. Recovery is not returning to the old normal—it is finding a new normal, a richer, deeper, and more conscious way of living. Our loved ones continue to guide us, and our grief becomes the teacher that leads us back to life.

I hope you carry forward the essence of these lessons: to love fully, to notice deeply, to grieve with honesty, and to remain open to the unseen. Life will continue to surprise you, challenge you, and teach you. But now, you can face it with the knowledge that grief, love, and connection are not obstacles—they are pathways to the most profound truths of existence.

Take them with you. Treasure them. And remember: the lessons from our grief teacher are never truly over—they are yours to live, and share your discovery with those you continue to commune with in this physical world. A conversation we must have to change the current trajectory in our communities that grief should be hidden. Let's bring it out of the shadows no matter how uncomfortable, to get to the conversations that connect us all as humans.

My hope is simple – we continue to discover our own truth and be open to the conversations with others about theirs.

A Grief Even Deeper

There is a grief that is hidden deep in the shadows of a victims life. For some the death of their family member, was met with shame or relief. For the person they buried was someone they loved for a relational reason but it was also someone they didn't like, feared or even hated.

Lauren Exposed

Lauren was a 48-year-old woman who's husband died 10 months prior to our first meeting. She had been marred to her husband since she was 18 and he was 26 years her senior. The reason she married so young was to escape an abusive environment. Her husband promised he would take care of her and in the first couple of decades he did just that. It wasn't ideal but it was better than the home she broke free from.

Her initial concern she shared with me is that since her husband died she was unable to sleep. She lied awake at night tossing and turning with thoughts and memories that appeared to cause her discomfort. I encouraged her to see her primary care physician to address her physical symptoms of insomnia and anxiety. Never forgo this step in your grief work. If you are having physical symptoms, and even though they can easily be attributed to your grief they should not be neglected as solely emotional responses. Your doctor should be included in your grief care so you do not overlook your total well-being.

Lauren did see her doctor. He prescribed some sleeping pills and anti-anxiety which she refused to take. I could tell there was something more to her story that she was struggling to share. With my best efforts I tried to get Lauren to open up. Her answers to my questions were always short and to the point with no elaboration. I provided her techniques to assist with sleeping such as meditation, creating an environment of comfort and playing soft music. I even suggested eating a slice of turkey before bed due to its tryptophan content.

She never said one derogatory word against her husband. I assumed they had a loving relationship but more on the stoic side.

One day I introduced her to a gratefulness technique. While this technique may seem too simple to be effective, studies have shown that gratitude improves mental health. Regularly practicing gratitude takes focus away from the negativity bias (focusing on what's wrong) and trains the brain to notice what is positive. It can reduce stress and boost neurotransmitters. Even if you initially do not feel grateful the practice of even finding the smallest things to be grateful for can help you move to a increased positive perspective. It improves self esteem and enhances emotional resilience.

As I was giving her examples, she tearfully excused herself and went into the kitchen. Lauren was a private crier, a trait I share, so I thought I would just sit quietly until she returned. Quite some time had passed so I respectfully went to the kitchen and gently asked if she was ok. Bursting with emotion, she said "No. I'm not ok. I can't be grateful. I am angry. I am so damn angry." I stood by as she paced the kitchen floor pouring out her withheld feelings. Her husband abused her, cheated on her, was diagnosed with dementia where she was forced to be his caregiver and then died leaving her penniless and she was facing losing her home.

Lauren went on for a couple of hours expressing her pain, suffering, and shaming herself for speaking ill of the dead.

Not all grief is love infused. For many their grief is embedded with ugly memories and heart wounds left open and bleeding. Unaddressed, with now no possibility of reconciliation or any type of closure. Lauren couldn't sleep because of her anger. She relived her abuse in her dreams, only to be awakened by the fear of her current circumstances. She revealed that parts of her were absolutely relieved that her husband was dead and quickly shuttered by the shame she felt through her acknowledgment.

Grief for Lauren was not easily addressed by leaning in and finding a continued love connection with her husband. She did not want that connection. She feared that connection.

I provided Lauren a referral to a licensed psycho therapist that could address her complex issues and address any mental health concerns. She did go but asked for me to continue to visit to coach her through navigating the waves of grief on a daily basis. Eventually Lauren found the piece she deserved. She did find that her grief offered her the opportunity to find herself again. Where she was silenced before, her pain through grief was so great it demanded expression.

She reconnected with herself and had a renewed spiritual awakening that had been severed by her anger that God never came to her rescue when she called on *Him*. She learned that the power always resided in her own self worth first. That the power of God, your source lies within you. Not some obscure guy in the sky with rope to pull you out.

The connection Lauren discovered through her grief was not with her husband but with herself. She learned her life had great value and she learned how powerful loving herself could be. Overtime she gained a new perspective. She was able to see how the story of her old self unfolded. She was able to find peace with her trauma that was now over and renew relationships with her remaining family that was strained.

I really admire Lauren. How she faced her deep, tragic grief which in time brought her new life.

What was possible for Lauren is also possible for you. If you resonate with Lauren's story please stop reading now and seek help. It is imperative for your well being. You are not expected to be alone in your complicated grief. For resources go to BalanceInGrief.com or check with your local hospice or Primary Care Physician for referrals.

Can you acknowledge now that grief is not just the residual pain you are left with after a loss. There is more to your story and your loved ones, than just a tragic end.

Allowing grief to be your teacher gives us the lessons we didn't know we needed to learn

Lesson 14
Homework

Part of my grief work has been learning about the brain and its natural process. I am not an expert in this area; however, even basic knowledge on how we process thoughts has proven itself to be helpful, especially during the grieving process.

In lay terms, this is some information on how your brain works. There are networks in your brain. One—The Default Mode Network (DMN). The DMN is the system active during rest, or shall we say unintentional thinking. It is your internal thoughts, like remembering the past, planning the future, daydreaming, self-reflection, observing the external world, and random thoughts. It is the brain's "autopilot." When someone says, I can't shut my brain off. They are correct. None of us can. Nor would we want to. However, sometimes the constant barrage of thought without elective meaning can create problems for us, such as difficulty sleeping, overthinking problems, or anxiety, just to name a few.

We may often tell ourselves, "I just have to get my mind off of things" and perhaps pursue a task or activity. This ignites the Task Positive Network (TPN). TPN is intentional thinking. It is purposefully constructive. It can be as simple as counting to 100 or as complex as inventing a machine. Shifting into TPN can assist you when the DMN has pushed you over into ruminating negative thoughts that are hindering you. That's why we count sheep to go to sleep.

In grief, ruminating thoughts are natural and common. Everyone gets stuck in negative loops, but when it is left unattended, it becomes persistent and interferes with life. It is a maladaptive pattern and can be a difficult habit to break. A habit that propels your grief into unnecessary suffering.

Mindfulness and meditation help to activate the TPN, which involves focused attention and executive control, quieting the mind-wandering of the DMN. It improves focus, reduces rumination, and promotes calm. Engaging the TPN through mindfulness and meditation releases dopamine while increasing other feel-good chemicals like serotonin, which helps to regulate emotions and reduce stress (lowering cortisol). It can improve attention, decision-making, and better emotional regulation.

Sometimes we may entertain a false belief that we should not allow ourselves to feel better while grieving. After all, our loved one has died, and we should feel miserable because of it. This is self-sabotage at its finest. The greatest lie in all of grief. Is this what you want for those that survive your death? Do you want them to suffer needlessly? Grief is hard enough without giving yourself up to be slaughtered. If there is no other message you receive from this book than "it's OK to pursue feeling better and to take care of you," then every word written was worth it.

This chapter's lesson is dedicated to teaching you how to begin to feel better by utilizing mindfulness, meditation, and gratefulness practices that will assist you through your grief course.

Mindfulness: Learning to Stay, When You Want to Escape

Mindfulness is the practice of noticing what is happening right now, without trying to change it. In grief, this can feel terrifying. Being present means feeling what hurts.

But avoiding the present is what keeps grief stuck. Stuck in grief eventually washes away all the vitality that you and your loved one ignited in each other. You are going to want to keep every precious gift you shared in this life with your loved one to the present. My dad used to sing goofy songs at random, stirring laughter and joy in my young heart. I think of him every time I share my goofy songs with my grandchildren. Now my grief is unstuck and living in the giggles of a new precious moment that my grandchildren will remember.

Mindfulness can be practiced anywhere. While washing dishes, walking, driving, or sitting quietly. It simply asks that you bring your attention to what you are doing, sensing, or feeling at this moment.

You might notice:

- *the weight of your body in the chair*
- *the sound of your breath*
- *the ache in your chest*
- *the warmth of sunlight on your skin*

You don't need to analyze any of it. Just notice.

When emotions arise, mindfulness invites you to say to yourself, *"This is sadness"* or *"This is longing,"* rather than *"This is unbearable."* Naming the experience creates distance from it. You are no longer swallowed by the emotion—you are observing it. It won't stop the feeling, nor do you want it to. You don't want to swallow your feelings. You want to give them space to be expressed.

The benefit of mindfulness in grief work is **integration**. Instead of suppressing pain or being consumed by it, mindfulness teaches you to walk alongside your grief. You learn that emotions move. They rise, peak, and fall. They do not destroy you.

Dr. Jill Bolte Taylor, a Harvard trained neuroanatomist explains in her book *My Stroke of Insight*, that the biological rise, peak, and fall of an *emotion's* initial chemical cascade is about 90 seconds. Yes, that's it... 90 seconds. However, the 90-second feeling is followed by thoughts and beliefs about what you are feeling. It is your **thoughts** that enhance the duration of the feeling into emotion. Understanding this information and utilizing mindfulness can help you move through unbearable feelings more quickly.

For example, I feel hurt. That feeling alone rises. My mind recognizes this feeling. It may be followed by a physical reaction such as feeling flush or tears, a pit in your stomach. In mindfulness you do not resist those feelings. You notice them. You do not judge them, and you do not add continued thoughts to them. Just feel it until it passes.

We generally add another thought to "*I feel hurt*" such as "*I can't stand it.*" Then we add another thought and another. We can stay in the loop of these thoughts for hours and days or longer. It starts like this:

I feel hurt. I can't stand it. How could she leave me? Look at all I am left with to try and figure it out on my own. No one can help me. I feel sick to my stomach. What am I expected to do now, and so on and so on.

We actually can talk ourselves into great uncertainty, anxiety, and depression, leading to physical pain because we continue to ruminate over these thoughts.

Mindfulness, when practiced, will eventually stop the momentum. You will learn to catch these cascading thoughts and release them. This reduces the intensity of the feeling. Some day with a continued mindfulness practice, you will replace those spinning thoughts like this:

I feel hurt.
I can't stand it.
How could she leave me?
I know she didn't want to.
We were so good together.
I am so lucky to have had her here with me and know her love.

See the difference? Yes, it will take practice. But relief and recovery from the pain of grief is worth it. Mindfulness builds trust—in your mind-body connection, in your resilience, and in your ability to be present for your own life again.

To get started with your mindfulness practice, set aside time where you are comfortable and just notice what is around you. Notice differing objects, their colors, and their texture. Notice any distinguishable scents. Notice what your skin is feeling, the clothes on your body, or the breeze on your face. Take note of what you like and don't like. Just be aware and observe. Don't ask the question why. Do this for a few minutes several times a day.

As you do that, notice how you feel. Again, don't ask why. Try to notice as many feelings as you can. I feel sad, I feel lonely, I feel warm, and I feel comfortable. Notice that good feelings, can accompany bad feelings. Bad feelings typically without a mindfulness practice, will tell you they are the only ones that exist. But that is simply not true. You can feel bad and good at the same time. Notice where you focus the most.

I feel sad.
I feel lonely
I feel comfortable
I feel safe

You can feel all the above at the same time. However, our focus is most often drawn only to the negative feelings in grief. Mindfulness helps you to identify all your feelings and encourages you to spend time with feelings that promote well-being.

Practicing mindfulness routinely will create a new normal for you that can achieve overall wellness and a platform for discovery. It will introduce what is possible for you and increase the connection between you and those around you.

Meditation: Learning there is More than What Meets the Eye

When you are grieving, your mind rarely rests. It circles the same thoughts, memories, regrets, and fears as if repetition might somehow change the outcome. Meditation does not ask you to stop grieving. It asks you to stop fighting yourself while you grieve.

Meditation is not about sitting a certain way, emptying your mind, or becoming spiritually advanced. It is simply the practice, like mindfulness, of creating a space where you allow yourself to be present with what is, without judgment, but for extended periods of time. Mindfulness is the awareness of the present moment. Meditation is generally designated time with the intent to achieve clarity, self-awareness, increased focus, reduced stress and inner peace. It also promotes overall well-being and emotional balance with deeper practices aiming for spiritual insight or liberation from suffering.

To begin, you don't need anything special. You don't need a designated space only for meditation with a pillow and chimes. You don't need long stretches of time or a specific regimen. Start small—five to ten minutes is enough. Sit or lie down in a position that is comfortable. Close your eyes, not to shut out the world, but to soften your attention from anything else. Bring your awareness to your breath. You don't need to control it. Just notice it.

Your thoughts will come. They always do, especially in grief. Memories, questions, anger, longing—none of this means you're doing it wrong. When a thought appears, notice it, and gently let it pass without engaging it. No mental commentary. No judgment. Just return to your breath or the stillness of the moment. That's it. That's how to begin meditation.

For some it may be helpful to have a focal point. This can be your breath or the noise of the air conditioner or a light instrumental in the background. When a thought appears, let it go and softly bring your focus back to your focal point. Try to stay focused on your focal point as long as possible.

Do not criticize yourself if you begin to get lost in your thoughts. This happens to everyone. That's why meditation is called a practice— because you have to practice. When you realize you have drifted, just ease your mind and go back to your focal point, and this will slow your thoughts down. The more you practice, you will find it becomes easier.

The benefit of meditation in grief work is not peace at first—it's **space**. Space between you and the pain. Space between the thought and the spiral. Over time, meditation teaches your nervous system that it is safe to rest, even in sorrow. It gives your mind and body a break from the constant strain of holding everything together.

Eventually, meditation becomes a place where grief can soften—not disappear, but breathe. It becomes a place where connection, insight, and comfort can arise naturally, without force. You will find the more you practice and find the moments of relief from grief, you will begin to crave it, and you will create more opportunities to practice.

Gratefulness: Learning to Find Light Without Dismissing the Dark

Gratitude can feel offensive when you are grieving. It can sound like denial or pressure to "look on the bright side." That is not what this practice is about.

Gratitude in grief is not about being thankful *for* the tragedy. It is about being present *with* life as it continues to unfold. As we spoke of in the mindfulness section, you can feel good and bad at the same time. This is helpful to bring balance to your mind-body connection for overall well- being.

A gratitude practice can begin very simply. Once a day—perhaps in the morning or before you go to sleep—pause and name three things you are grateful for. Write them down. Just three. It can be as small as a warm cup of coffee, a moment of quiet, a memory that made you smile, warm socks, or the fact that you got through the day.

It is not necessary to *feel* grateful. In fact, you won't 'feel it' initially. Practicing gratitude routinely and daily is helping you to notice that there is more than just your grief. It is creating a pattern that steadies your thoughts and keeps you from sinking. Balance in grief is extremely important.

Some days, gratitude might feel impossible. On those days, gratitude can sound like this:

I am grateful I survived today.
I am grateful I loved deeply enough to hurt this much.
I am grateful I only have to think of three things. (That counts.)

The benefit of gratitude in grief work is that it gently retrains your attention. Grief narrows our focus to what is gone. Gratitude widens it just enough to remind us that life, love, and connection still exist alongside the pain.

Over time, gratitude does not diminish grief—it **balances** it. It allows sorrow and appreciation to coexist. And in that coexistence, the heart begins to expand rather than harden.

Years ago my daughter was in a bad accident. She was in the hospital for well over a week, away from her two kids, and she was going through a painful divorce. She was laid off from work, and the future was an extremely frightening prospect. I encouraged her to start a gratefulness journal. "Just 3 things you're grateful for today." As she began her practice, it wasn't long before she was able to fill a page of things she was grateful for even in the midst of her tragic circumstances. It grounded her, encouraged her, and gave her time away from her negative thoughts. It balanced her perspective to the point she felt hopeful again. It is a practice she continues to this day.

I know it sounds too simple or too easy to offer any kind of real help during grief. That may be so, but statistically the evidence is unquestionable. According to the research from Mental Health First Aid and the Journal of Positive Psychology, a gratefulness practice has been linked to a 35% reduction in depressive symptoms. That's significant.

What do you have to lose to try? It is simple and worth it.

Practices for Grief
Mindfulness, meditation, and gratefulness are not separate from grief. They are ways of listening to what grief is trying to teach.

They teach you how to pause instead of react.
How to soften instead of harden.
How to stay connected—to yourself, to others, and to your loved one—without needing to escape the pain.

You do not need to master these practices. You only need to return to them, again and again, just as the waves and triggers of grief return to you.

Viewing grief as a teacher promotes your ability to make a choice for yourself through every daunting wave and piercing trigger. I am not trying to put a mask on grief and call it something it's not by offering remedies to the pain. I am however, hoping you will see that your grief is a common thread in humanity, like being born. This vast shared experience has to have a reason for being. And while you think you have lost yourself in the process, it can offer you lessons in love and life.

Grief is not asking you to become someone else. It is asking you to become more present to who you already are. And that, perhaps, is the deepest lesson of all.

Lesson 15
Questions for the Teacher

When it comes to learning lessons, what was your favorite subject in school? What was the class you looked forward to the most? What are the things you love to do now and would love to learn more about? What are your interests? When you have a subject or interest that is important to you, it makes a difference in the quality of your life. Grief may not have been the teacher you wanted, but it does have the lessons we need to learn to improve our perspective on the deeper aspects of life and the afterlife.

I was a music and drama teacher for a private school my kids attended for a couple of years during their elementary and junior high school years. As I mentioned earlier, I have always loved teaching. Mostly because teachers get to learn more. For my students, my mission for each student was to *learn to love to learn* more than just teaching facts. My hope was to inspire them to discover their own unique talents and seek their own education as they continued in their years to come. Asking themselves questions about why they loved certain subjects and to always pursue their interests.

Now as a grief coach I realize, though the subject is difficult, the mission is the same: learn to love to learn. Be inspired to discover what may have never crossed your mind before. The discussion of grief is not a subject that becomes anyone's favorite subject. As a child, I never thought, *When I grow up, I want to be a grief counselor*. It really isn't on anyone's radar to choose a path blanketed in sadness and despair. Those who have chosen this path were led there by their own grief teacher. I was clearly the student who didn't want to engage in this class. Now that I have, it has truly left me wanting to learn more. I have become so curious about why I am here, what the point of life is, where I am going, and what is beyond the veil between life and physical death.

I am inspired to ask more questions and have the unwanted conversations that unify and bring healing.

The little girl in me had so many questions that apparently no adult in my life had the answers to. Or maybe the answers they knew for themselves were not satisfying their own lack of understanding, and the conversation was much too daunting. However, having the willingness to say, '*I don't know that answer*," is so much better than the alternatives. Making stuff up or answering a question with platitudes instead of the raw truth.

It has been my experience that meeting with those who grieve through my own vulnerability without preconceived notions or expectations and with an open heart of empathy provides a connection with the assurance that the bereaved can speak directly from their anguish and feel safe from judgment. Some of our bereaved community and this may include you, are desperately looking for support for a loneliness in their heart that is incomparable.

Traumatic Loss

I had a dear friend whose daughter was brutally raped and killed at age 19. She was a beautiful girl away on training for the new career she was pursuing. Staying in a local extended-stay hotel, she was found naked and bloody in the bathroom.

Again, what is the answer to this question of why? There are no words. Even emotional outcries are not satisfying for this type of anguish.

The church community surrounded my friend with great prayer and benevolence. All of which was appreciated and yet completely discomforting, only because her pain could not be soothed. While we all gathered around her as best we knew how, it was an indescribable tragedy with no answers to any questions.

I sat with my friend one day on a bench near her gravesite, where she began to pour out her absolute horror and disgust over the things people would say to her. Things like *Your daughter is a beautiful angel in heaven now. God must have wanted her to be with him. Someday you will see her again. Just be grateful she's in heaven. You have other kids to love.*

I do believe these comments, while well-intended, are like pouring salt into a wound. No words are better than what she was given. A quiet presence in empathy would be a better offering. Perhaps words that are better shared would sound something like this: *I love you. I'm sorry. When you are able, make a list of things you need done, and I will take care of it right away.* Practical support can go a longer way in being supportive rather than words.

As she was relieving some of her frustration and anger, I couldn't help but feel that God was angry too. God did not allow this to happen—a brutal beast did. God does not just want to snatch a girl from her loving family and hopeful future to have for *Himself* in heaven. That makes no sense at all. Why would God, who is

the source of love and well-being, do that? That
was my friend's question.

*Without a second thought, I responded with, "I
think Jesus thinks this is totally f*cked up too."*
She responded loudly,

"Yes, yes, yes!!!! I do too."

She was more consoled by my coarse phrase
revealing that God was not a sadistic maniac,
"allowing" such a horrific assault to take place
just so He could have another angel in heaven.
Again, while the "*why*" cannot be fully known,
the **"how's"** can begin a work that will change
the inner sanctum of your soul. *How* can I go
on? *How* can I stay connected?

It's important to note that in grief, we will
have questions that we cannot answer.
Especially right away after death. The higher
learning of grief is not for the faint of heart, and
it is a lifelong journey. Why is there so much
war, evil, and death in the world...? I do not
know. Nobody knows. That is the fact.
However, working on the questions of *how we
can help those who are in war-torn territories,
How can we combat the evil in the world and
provide protection* gives a directive to deepen
our life experiences in the midst of our grief.

What I do know is that in this world, as I
have shared before, there is a dichotomy we all
must navigate. None of us escapes the highs and

the lows. Why do some people go through more devastation in their lives than others? I don't know, and I cannot believe that a supreme being is handing out life sentences, and we are just stuck with whatever we get. It may feel that way, but that cannot be the total answer.

The questions in grief are profound and most often only lead to more questions. Some of my questions are, why aren't we allowing ourselves these conversations around our shared grief? What is your experience with grief? How do you feel going through this traumatic time? What will make you feel better, if anything, right now? What are the ways to find some relief in this moment?

The questions I am more interested in asking as time goes on are: How do I feel the continued connection with my loved ones? Are they able to connect with me? How does our higher intelligence, supreme being, source, or God figure into all of this? How do I see the perspective from my loved one's point of view so I can better understand the value of this life I am still living? How can I expand my love to those who are living in this physical world now? How can we reconcile that we have choices in this life regarding how we continue to live, grieve, or suffer? Am I stronger than I know? Will I let the status quo, false beliefs, and avoided questions keep me hostage in my own life, or will I rise from the ashes of pain and help others to rise too? Is grieving together how we begin to heal the world?

Dare I say the answer may be answered with the question. *It's not what you think?* Let's break out of the school of thought we have placed ourselves in to discover answers beyond our current beliefs.

For the bereaved, this will be a lifelong conversation. Grief breaks down every boarded-up door and window you try to nail closed into your heart. The pressure from your emotions is the powerful waves of grief that flood you when you least expect it.

Just When You Think Your Doing Fine

Thirteen years after my mom died, I would have said I was doing quite well. I was busy raising 3 kids and active in my usual routines as a wife and mother. I was walking in the center of a mall, running errands, when I noticed a woman who was my same age. Packages in hand, she was happily strolling alongside, chatting away, obviously, with her mom. They looked quite alike and appeared to be enjoying each other's company through their loving exchanges.

I had a couple more stops to make in the mall, but my feet wouldn't move. I was stopped in my tracks, staring at these two women. I could feel heat rising from my gut that was now turning with nausea. My face became flushed, and I could feel myself trembling inside. Tears welled up in my eyes, falling down my cheeks to the point that my view became blurry. I took a deep breath and forced myself to move, running out of that mall as fast as I could. I jumped in my car, locked the doors behind me, and sobbed like I never had before.

What was wrong with me? It was a frenzy of emotion that was so unexpected, uncontrolled, and unstoppable. I couldn't get it together. My vocal cords made a roar from the deep ache in the depths of my soul—it was grief's sledgehammer dismantling the walls I had built it in my heart and mind.

I realized in a swift moment in that mall, I would never be an adult woman, enjoying a wonderful day with my mom.

This is called a STUG reaction. Sudden Trigger Urge of Grief. They are just as I described: unexpected, uncontrolled, and unstoppable.

As time has marched on, I have since become that mom to my adult children that I had witnessed that day in the mall. Enjoying and valuing my time with them in a deeper way than they may even understand, not having experienced the loss of me. I try not to hold on too tightly in fear I will lose them, because that would ruin it all. I take each moment as it comes with gratefulness, as my teacher has taught me to do.

Grief, the teacher, can show you how to live if you allow it. It will reveal to you many opportunities to learn, grow, and lead a magical life if you are willing to engage its invitation. I say magical because while missing the tangibility of my loved ones, I feel a much deeper conversation with them now. It's not so much with words, although I can get a bit chatty; it's more of a knowing.

When I approach the veil and allow myself to feel them loving me, I know what they would say in that moment. I have a collective of guides that embrace me through the rugged terrain of this physical life. I become aware of nuances, the subtle beauty that this life has to offer. I feel their strength when I am weak, and my faith in the Source and the knowledge of the true messages of the great masters in spirit, have become amplified and revolutionary to my own journey.

I don't settle for not knowing. I press in to know more. Mindfulness, meditation, and gratefulness have become daily tools that I continue to practice to press in closer to the unknown. If I have learned one thing about grief for sure —I will never graduate. There is no end to this class. There is always more to learn. I have learned to love learning about life – because of my lessons in death. Grief does not have to be your demise. With more conversation, support and the courage to ask questions, you can have the grief relief you

desperately are seeking. Your tears do not have
to turn into despair. Your focus does not have to
be only on the death but should free you to see a
perspective of life unavailable to you before. I
will not say grief is the gift of death. I
emphatically am saying it is **not** a gift. But grief
is a looking glass into a part of life we couldn't
see before.

Please continue to join me by beginning to
discover what is possible for you. Don't be shy
and hide or bury your feelings of grief. Feel the
pain so that when relief comes, and it will, you
will feel its calm peace. Press into the new
discoveries about yourself, your spirit, and your
loved ones' continued journey beyond. Don't be
tethered to beliefs that no longer serve you. I
trust that all that you have faith in will multiply
if you're willing to let go of what is holding you
back from your growth.

We, who are bereaved, are a loving, genuine,
vulnerable, raw, strong, brave community who
need to not only support each other but also
teach those who will join our classroom. Grief is
a unifying commonality in the human race.
Remember it's not only grief from death but so
many other challenges too. As we learn to grieve
together —we will also learn to recover together.

My heartfelt empathy is with you.
Know you are never alone.
They are just across a thin veil.

BalanceInGrief.com

About the Author

Kat Farace

At just **11 years old**, Kat Farace began facing a series of losses that would shape the rest of her life. Between the ages of **11 and 30**, she experienced the deaths of **14 family members and close friends**, each one teaching her lessons about love, resilience, and the ways grief can both break and transform us.

These early experiences, combined with over **25 years of hospice and end-of-life care**, have given Kat a rare perspective on grief—as both a deeply personal journey and a universal human experience. She has walked alongside thousands of individuals and families, helping them navigate the profound realities of death, loss, and bereavement with compassion, honesty, and presence.

Kat is an author, speaker, and grief coach whose work centers on **holding space for grief, honoring loss, and helping others find meaning and hope in the midst of sorrow**. She lives a life devoted to listening, learning, and walking alongside others as they discover the lessons that only love and loss can teach.

Let's Stay Connected

Thank you for walking through *Grief the Teacher* with me. Writing this book was a deeply personal journey, and I hope somewhere in these pages you felt seen, supported, and less alone. If you would like continued support, I would love to stay connected.

Website: **balanceingrief.com**
Instagram & TikTok: **@BalanceInGrief**
Facebook: **BalanceInGrief**
YouTube: **Balance In Grief with Kat Farace**

On my website, you'll find free grief tip sheets, my free newsletter, and information about Grief Coaching.

B.E.S.T. Results Grief Work
For those wanting deeper, structured support, I created the **B.E.S.T. Results Grief Work Curriculum** and companion **B.E.S.T. Results Reflective Workbook**.

B.E.S.T. stands for:
Brain – How you process thoughts and emotions.
Examine – Your beliefs about grief.
Self-Care – Caring for yourself intentionally.
Techniques – Practical tools for daily living
Learn more at **balanceingrief.com**.

Coming Soon

If you benefitted from Grief the Teacher, I would like you to know that I am currently writing another book about grief and our eternal connection. Planned for release later this year. Join my newsletter at **balanceingrief.com** to keep updated on its progress and release, as well as other products.

Thank you for allowing me to share my story with you. It is an honor to walk beside you in yours.

With warmth and gratitude,

Kat

The text of Grief the Teacher was entirely
written by the author. No artificial intelligence
was used in the writing of this manuscript.

The cover art was created with the assistance of
AI tools.